PRAISE FOR *GRACE, NOT PERFECTION*

"In some of the most grace-filled words I have ever encountered, Emily Ley offers women a much-needed exhale and permission to be a priority. *Grace, Not Perfection* is the end of depleted, maxed-out, and unfulfilled days and the beginning of realistic standards that allow you to joyfully live and breathe."

—RACHEL MACY STAFFORD
New York Times bestselling author of *Hands Free Mama* and *Hands Free Life*

"*Grace, Not Perfection* is a must-read for all women. Whether you are a mom, student, sister, or wife, Emily has written a book for all of us who struggle with letting go of perfection. Practical and beautifully written, *Grace, Not Perfection* gives us the freedom to make what matters happen and to step into a life of purpose. Get ready for a joy-filled journey as you turn each page!"

—LARA CASEY
author of *Make It Happen* and *Cultivate*

"Women across America, myself included, have watched Emily Ley's story unfold, and they've wondered, "How does she do it all?" This book is the gracious and life-giving answer to that question. Emily steps down off the pedestal that so many women put her on to give a vibrant, honest, and wisdom-filled answer for our generation. Her strategies will make *simplicity* and *prioritizing* your two favorite words, and you'll feel renewed purpose to do the things you're meant to do—with a huge blessing to throw off the notion that you must do it all. Thank you, Emily, for this book!"

—JESS CONNOLLY
coauthor of *Wild and Free*, women's speaker

"From the outside, it looks like Emily does everything beautifully and does it well. This book, however, also gives you a look into the heart of the woman who helps thousands of women plan their days. For this reformed perfectionist, this book hits all the right notes. It's a grace-filled invitation to let go of do-it-all and step into a simpler, more gracious way of living—more margin, more truth, more heart."

—HAYLEY MORGAN

coauthor of *Wild and Free* and cofounder of The Influence Conference

"This book speaks to the soul. It's a must-read for all women, especially moms and entrepreneurs!"

—COURTNEY WHITMORE

cookbook author and blogger at pizzazzerie.com

"*Grace, Not Perfection* has been a lullaby to me at the end of each day as I read in bed, weary from the challenges of the day behind me. As I turned each page, I would feel the weight of the day leaving me. The warmth in Emily's words felt like the comfort of a sage older sister pointing me back to my Father, to a God who is so much bigger than my plans and, thankfully, in complete control when I feel the darkness of stress and worry creeping into my heart. It's difficult to feel that we can actually give ourselves grace in the middle of so much hustle, but it's necessary. And absolutely possible."

—ERIN NAPIER

host of HGTV's *Home Town* and owner of Lucky Luxe

Presented to:

_____

From:

_____

Date:

_____

grace not Perfection

embracing **SIMPLICITY**, *celebrating* **JOY**

EMILY LEY

THOMAS NELSON
Since 1798

To Brady, Tyler,
and Caroline—
be still and know.
You are deeply loved
just as you are.

CONTENTS

CONTENTS

INTRODUCTION

I'M SO HONORED THAT my book found its way into your hands. I know firsthand that the hamster wheel of trying to do it all is an exhausting place to be. I understand the circus—because as a wife, mom of three, business owner, designer, and hopeless overachiever, I am living it. I know how difficult and fast and overwhelming life can be when you want it *all* and want to do it all perfectly. I know those aches of your heart. I know that you were probably going in ten different directions as fast as you could today and picked this book up in search of a little relief from it all. Thank you for letting me share my story and what I've learned along the way with you. Let's pretend we're having coffee at your local coffee shop. I'll share my journey with you and give some tactical tips along the way. But this book isn't just about me. This book is about *you*—the deepest, most sincere desires of your heart. We'll walk through interactive checklists, questions, and strategies. Be prepared—we'll laugh too. If I've learned anything, it's that having a sense of humor amid the craziness is crucial.

Although my degrees are in English and public administration, I decided to follow a dream. I Googled many questions in the wee hours of the morning while working two full-time jobs and taught myself to be a designer. In 2011, after the birth of my first son, I created the Simplified Planner®—a simple agenda designed very minimally on purpose, to give busy women a tactical, fresh start every day. Since then, my tiny idea has grown into a product line sold in hundreds of stores around the world, and my solo operation has grown into a team of six incredibly talented women. My family has grown as well—with twins. I am so humbled and honored to share my journey with you. It's not a perfect one, but looking back, I can see God perfectly orchestrating every failure and milestone into a song of daily surrender and joy.

As a designer, I am very concerned with image, with crafting seamless, consistent messaging and perfectly tweaked visuals. Without a doubt, that bleeds into my personal life. I know what the chase to "have it all together" does to a girl who has big dreams and simply wants to be the best she can be. And I've learned (by falling on my face quite a few times) that being perfect isn't really all it's cracked up to be, that real life is so much richer. Throughout these pages, we'll explore what it takes to live in an authentic state of grace that lets you escape those feelings of endless struggle and defeat—the ones we often cover over with a carefully constructed image. Together, we'll take a look at practical steps you can take to free your mind from Pinterest perfection and have grace with yourself. We'll dig in to the struggles we all face as we try to be our best for our people, and we'll discuss strategies for delivering and receiving grace within those circles. And lastly, we'll explore what it means to step into your true calling in a way that allows you to be your best, most real, most joyful self. In a world that holds us up to a standard of perfection at every turn, you can find something better: grace.

Part 1

GRACE WITH YOURSELF

SOMEWHERE ALONG THE WAY, someone told us we weren't good enough. We weren't pretty enough, creative enough, crafty enough, or dedicated enough. Social media feeds, blogs, magazines, and other people began to set the standard for us. And they set it *high*—unreachably high. We mashed together other people's highlights and best moments and created this standard of perfection we're all after. *Once I reach it*, we tell ourselves, *I'll be good enough. I'll be a good mom, a good friend, a good spouse, a good professional.*

Birthday parties are now judged by Pinterest-worthiness—that picture-perfect quality that people swoon over online. Dress sizes are measures of our physical worth—the smaller, the better. And busyness? Well, that's just the norm. We run on adrenaline and lattes. If we're not busy, then we're not measuring up. At least that's what we've told ourselves. And although the chase may earn us "likes" and immaculate Instagram photos, it also leaves us feeling empty, alone, and just plain not good enough. So we try to do it all: we answer e-mails and push baby swings. We text and drive. We over-load, overcommit, overwork, and end up overwhelmed.

Without realizing it, many of us have decided to let the world tell us what the "good life" looks like. And, sister, this isn't it. The perfectly constructed, magazine-worthy life does not equal happiness. Happiness isn't found in the prettiest Instagram feed or in a large number of Facebook friends. True joy isn't found in having it all together. The good life is rich, slow, real, and flawed.

Forget what the world is telling you. You don't have to con-stantly strive to be more. *You are enough.* You deserve simple, slow, and sweet. You are worthy of happiness. You deserve silly, extravagant joy, belly laughs, and rich memories worthy of being slowly retold in rocking chairs on front porches. This is attainable—where you are, as you are, with what you have right now. And together, through the next few chapters, we're going to talk through simple, practical ways to attain this.

Chapter 1

DISCOVERING GRACE

For it is by grace you have been saved,
through faith—and this is not from
yourselves, it is the gift of God.

EPHESIANS 2:8

IT WAS LATE AFTERNOON, and traffic in Tampa was disastrous. I was racing home to get ready for date night after a big day at work. Hours before, I had nervously and triumphantly handed in my two weeks notice. It was official: I was leaving the corporate world to dive headfirst into the fledgling design business I'd nurtured in the wee hours for the previous two years. It was finally time to devote my attention to the endeavor that had stolen my heart and ignited my passions: designing meaningful paper goods for life's most special moments. Though I was eager to get home to celebrate, I spied

a drugstore ahead and turned in to the parking lot. Twizzlers suddenly sounded like a great idea.

This might be where all you mamas giggle and remember the first telltale sign of your pregnancy. Gracious. I should have known something was up! I'm normally a gummy bear girl.

I pulled into my driveway a few minutes later. The Twizzlers were long gone, but a pregnancy test was tucked away in my purse. Without much thought, I tossed my purse on the counter and took the test to the bathroom. I wanted to be sure I could safely enjoy a glass of celebratory champagne that evening. I had learned after months of disappointment not to put too much thought into those tests. Too much thought always equaled too much heartache.

I saw the ink begin to appear and impatiently set it aside. For such a small thing, that test packed a pretty big punch. It scratched at a very raw, painful spot in my heart that I desperately wanted to ignore on that happy day. Our years-long road of infertility had been paved with more bumps and potholes than we ever thought we'd face, and I wanted nothing more than to be a mama. Remembering that I'd purchased an unfamiliar drugstore brand, I picked the box up to read the instructions one more time.

Confused and suddenly breathless, I laid the test, the instructions, and the box next to my bathroom sink. I held the test next to the diagram on the crumpled paper and, in an instant, felt my heart begin to race and my breath leave my chest. I looked around the empty room, desperate for someone to run to, to scream with. Memories of pill bottles, doctor appointments, and infertility procedures flooded my head as tears gathered in my eyes. I heard Bryan's truck pull into the driveway as the tears fell down my cheeks. Though I'd scoured Pinterest for months for the perfect, photo-worthy way to tell him he'd be a daddy, I ran to him—a red-faced, tear-stained mess—and blurted it all out. "I don't . . . this thing . . . the Twizzlers . . ." I caught my breath through a beautiful, ugly cry. "A baby. I'm pregnant." It was perfect.

Becoming a mama on February 16, 2011, was the most pivotal experience of my life. My heart suddenly existed outside my body in this chubby little ball of all that is good in the world. Every emotion seemed heightened. Food tasted sweeter. Tiredness was now exhaustion. Love was a totally new feeling.

"I love him so much it physically hurts," I tearfully confessed to my own mom as she folded a tiny blue onesie and put it in Brady's dresser.

She paused and smiled. "That never changes."

These new emotions were confusing and overwhelming. I loved Brady with a new part of my heart—with feelings I'd never experienced before. I loved him with an all-encompassing love that I wondered if he'd ever understand.

Our new little guy didn't like to sleep. At all. During those late-night feedings, I'd search the Internet for all the ways to be a great mom: the best Facebook-worthy styled photos to capture his growth, the coolest toys around, the fanciest celebrity-designed nurseries, and the most dapper little-man outfits. One night, as Pinterest ran dry, I laid my phone on the armrest of the rocking chair and closed my eyes. *Exhausted* didn't even begin to describe how I felt. Brady had finally fallen asleep—his little head nuzzled into the space between my shoulder and chin. I breathed his sweet baby smell and prayed for him. And as I did, God laid an enormous truth on my heart: "I love you the same way, Emily. I get it."

GRACE

I tried for a long time to be the Pinterest-worthy girl with the Pinterest-worthy home and the Pinterest-worthy marriage and the Pinterest-worthy child. I wanted the world to know my life was pretty effortless and I had it all together. I wanted to be the girl people pointed out on Facebook and said, "Did you see that super-cute, over-the-top thing she did for her kid's birthday?" To me, that translated to, "Did you see how much she loves her child?" Sweet validation! *I'm doing a good job!* I'd think. *I must be—people I don't know very well approve of and admire me.*

It was a destructive way of thinking. I thought if I proved my worth by wearing the perfect clothes, having home-cooked dinners on the table at six, raising perfectly dressed children, and presenting a perfectly curated Instagram feed, I could finally rest. Then I could say, "I did it!" I would have earned the love and admiration of my friends, of my family, and of God.

To me, *perfect* meant my parents were proud. *Perfect* meant my husband was proud. *Perfect* meant my children were proud. I believed the lie that *perfect* meant I was worthy. It turns out, grace was already there to deliver me from that emptiness. I just hadn't realized it yet.

> *Perfect doesn't equal worthy.*

Here's the thing about grace: you don't have to be perfect to embrace it. Grace is *free*—for imperfect and unworthy people like you and me. Did you catch that? You don't have to be perfect! I don't either! Jesus took care of that for us. He went before us and made a way. While we are busy trying to plan extravagant birthday parties and have exquisitely put-together homes, God has set a standard totally outside our realm of thinking. Instead of calling us to be hopeless overachievers, he calls us to "walk by the Spirit . . . [with] love, joy, peace, forbearance, kindness, goodness, faithfulness, gentleness and self-control" (Galatians 5:16, 22–23). Nowhere in there did He mention perfect birthday parties, size 4 jeans, home-cooked dinners, or spotless homes.

In fact, I don't think God really cares a whole lot about all of that. God cares more about us abiding by His commandments and loving big—feeling deeply alive and free from the traps of perfection and comparison. He's watching us scurry about, saying, "Sweet girls, why are you so hard on yourselves? All this worry and busyness is for what? I've given you all you need."

God is pouring grace on us every day, abundantly and without restraint. So, sister, if God is giving us so much grace, why on earth aren't we having a little more grace with ourselves? Why are we running ourselves ragged trying to measure up? I don't know about you, but I find this rat race of ours exhausting. And it's really easy to feel like a hamster in a wheel chasing an impossible glossy-magazine standard we've set for ourselves. Grace, and only grace, offers us a way to step off that wheel—a deep breath, a place to rest, and the opportunity to slow down and savor what truly matters.

A STANDARD OF GRACE

I started to get my feet back under me post-maternity leave. Some days I felt like I had this new mom thing down, and other days I wanted to hide in the bathroom with a bag of gummy bears. Regardless, one year into life as a full-time designer, I was determined to prove to the world that I could do it all. But here's the thing about doing it all: even if you *can* do it all, no one can do it all *well*.

What

STANDARD

are you holding

yourself to?

Who defined

PERFECTION

for you?

I took client calls while nursing. I worked frantically during nap times. And playtime at the park was a regular event for the three of us—me, Brady, and my iPhone. Instead of enjoying the best parts of a job I loved and a child I adored, I burned my candle at both ends trying to keep up. You can imagine how far that got me. Still, I was determined that I didn't need help.

One morning, I paced a circle around my house attempting to multitask. I can still remember the sound my bare feet made on the laminate wood floor while I bounced three-month-old Brady in the carrier strapped to my stomach. I was helplessly trying to pacify him and answer a design client's questions about the breakdown of her new brand colors. I tried to sound peppy and focused so the client knew I was devoting all my attention to her, but Brady was clearly ready to be fed. After the call was over, a flood of tears and frustration washed over me.

I called my business partner and close friend, Lara Casey. "I can't do it," I told her matter-of-factly. "I'm failing at everything. Everything." Lara just listened. "I thought I could do it all. I thought I could be the picture-perfect mom running the picture-perfect business, but I'm just so tired. I haven't washed my hair in days. I'm failing everyone. I've got to find a new standard," I said. God had been pouring grace on me, but all I wanted to do was prove to the world that I could do it all. This was a breaking point. I was done. Feeling totally incapable of reaching the incredibly unattainable standard I'd set for myself, I laid it all on the table at this moment. Something had to give. My standard had to go.

I stopped bouncing and pacing in my bedroom next to a pile of clean, unfolded laundry. "I'm not doing this anymore," I told Lara. "I'm done trying to be everything to everyone, trying to prove a point to the world. I will not chase this impossible standard. I'll hold myself to a standard of grace, not perfection."

Imagine me stomping my foot on the floor while saying that, because that's the resolve I felt. Though I've fallen on my face daily since then, simply making that statement aloud freed my heart from a world of burdens. I'd honestly believed that being "put together" in every area of my life would equal happiness. Chasing perfection had been my way of searching for joy.

CHASING JOY

Have you ever visited Disney World with a three-year-old? You have to do it. To a three-year-old, everything is new and everything is exciting (until they melt down in front of Cinderella's Castle, but that's another story for another chapter). In early 2014, we took Brady to Disney World. I planned that trip months in advance, with attention to every detail so that it would be magical in every way. And Disney World didn't disappoint. Bryan and I took Brady to a live performance first

Here's the thing about doing it all:

even if you can do it all,

no one can do it all **WELL.**

thing in the morning. He was enamored with the characters and loved every minute of it. When Mickey Mouse himself came onto the stage in all his Disney glory, Brady jumped to his feet, threw his little arms high into the air, and gasped with the most electric, wide-eyed, genuine excitement I've ever seen. There's just nothing like a three-year-old meeting his beloved Mickey for the first time.

That's heart-bursting joy. That's what we're all after. Somewhere between three and twenty-, thirty-, and fortysomething (I left out fifty, because I'm convinced all the fifty-year-olds I know have this figured out), we lost that joy. And now we're all trying to find it again. Our grown-up circumstances, mortgages, taxes, jobs, and social media comparison have sucked the wind right out of our sails and made us all a little bit unhappy inside. And here we are, convinced that getting down to our college weight and a maintaining a spotless home sounds like a pretty good way to be unabashedly happy again. The truth is, if we take care of ourselves the same way we're nurturing everyone else, we'll find all sorts of joy and be better for everyone we love.

My come-to-Jesus moment with my baby strapped to my chest helped me realize that I needed to take care of myself or I'd have nothing left to give my little ones. It wasn't an indulgence or a pat on the back. It was do or die. If my heart was going to keep me going, it was going to need attention. It was time to give myself permission to be a priority again—starting *now*.

MY THOUGHTS

What does extravagant joy look like to you?
When was the last time you were esctatically happy?

No. 1

No. 2

No. 3

Chapter 2

THE EMPTY WELL

Above all else, guard your heart, for
everything you do flows from it.

PROVERBS 4:23

HOW ARE YOU? Like, how are you *really*?

My friend Lara asks me this question a lot, and I can always tell that she's ready for me to lay it all out for her. What a gift, to be able to spill your heart and be heard. So I'm asking you the same question. How are you? Take a minute and a deep breath. Consider the way your heart feels, the way your hands move, and the rhythm of your heartbeat.

How are you? Seriously . . .

_____

_____

_____

I'll start. I'm tired. After my first bundle of joy, I had twin babies. And they were both up last night. I had a hard time falling back asleep, worrying about one of them trying to climb out of the crib. I'm overwhelmed. I'm writing a book, preparing for the holidays, and designing next year's Simplified Planners at the same time. I skipped breakfast this morning and am functioning on one nonfat grande cappuccino. Sound familiar? My responsibilities seem crushing at times. I'm the caretaker of my family. I'm a mama. I run a company. I manage lunches and dinners and staff meetings and schedules and production calendars and playdates. I have a lot going on. I want to be everything to everyone, so I'm running on empty these days, even though I know better.

How do we even begin to have grace with ourselves in these situations? In my head, I know it means forgiving myself for my mess and finding peace in my circus. But if you're like me, you know it's easier said than done. It all comes down to this question: What good are we when we're overwhelmed, overbooked, and overcommitted?

You are a living, breathing vessel of love, sweet friend, and so am I. We need care, rest, nutrients, and full hearts to be able to speak life into the people we love.

Imagine a beautiful car created with precision, craftsman-ship, and attention to every tiny detail. The car is bright and shiny and beautiful its first trip around the block. But after a while, the car stops being a showpiece. It runs errands, shuffles kids back and forth to soccer practice, and endures rain, wind, snow, and mud. It gets bumped and scratched and left in the garage without washing. After a while, it's obvious the car needs a good wash and a tune-up, a refill of gas, and maybe a coat of wax, or the car isn't going to be good for anyone anymore.

Isn't that car just like you? If you run yourself ragged car-ing for everyone but yourself while expecting perfection from your hands, body, and mind, you're in for a rough collision with reality.

SWEET WATER

Okay, so we're not machines. We don't run on diesel, and we don't have an ignition switch (as much as we might like one). Our hearts are moving, loving, organic things. You might say our hearts are wells—deep and wide. If our well is not fed by a freshwater spring, where it can be replenished and refilled, we have no water to give to the ones we love. If our well is fed by a stream of comparison, anxiety, and stress, guess what we will have to give to our families? Sharp words, headaches, and impatience will brim at the top. Nothing good can come out of that poisoned well. But what would we have if we let our wells be filled with things like rest, laughter, confidence, good tea, hugs, and adventure? I want to overflow with that sweet water.

In Galatians, we read, "You, my brothers and sisters, were called to be free. But do not use your freedom to indulge the flesh; rather, serve one another humbly in love. For the entire law is fulfilled in keeping this one command: 'Love your neighbor as yourself'" (5:13–14). The last line of that passage is so powerful: love your neighbor *as yourself.* We usually think of that command as centering around others. But it's about us too. God is telling us to love, nurture, and care for ourselves and to love others that much as well. I don't know about you, but if I loved and nurtured my neighbor (or my children!) the same way I care for myself sometimes, I wouldn't be doing any of them a whole lot of good.

Before our twins were born, an average day at my house began with my three-year-old son, Brady, bounding into our bedroom bright-eyed, full of energy, and ready for the day. I, of course, had made sure he was in bed by eight the night before. Then I'd stayed up four more hours doing laundry, catching up on *Parenthood*, and clearing out my inbox to make sure the next day wouldn't escape me. Groggy, I'd pull

MY THOUGHTS

How can I care for myself?

No. 1

No. 2

No. 3

How can I care for others?

No. 1

No. 2

No. 3

myself from my bed and let him watch a cartoon while I fran-tically showered and threw on workout clothes. I typically had no plans to work out, but I always thought wearing workout clothes meant I was ready for anything. (Or maybe leggings and a T-shirt pulled from the hamper were all I had energy to pick out.) From that minute on, I played chase with my day and continually found myself ten steps behind. My outward appearance definitely matched the way I felt on the inside—frazzled and exhausted.

Why do women always put ourselves last? It's tragic, and I used to be a terrible offender. Women, showers are nonne-gotiable, and leggings are not pants. Makeup is optional, but sister, feed yourself breakfast (and not out of a mug)! You're doing no one any favors by putting yourself last. In fact, although you think you're doing the selfless thing by putting everyone else first, you're actually sabotaging all your efforts by refusing to take time to fill your tank.

Somewhere, some time ago, someone told you that you had to do it all—and that you had to do it all by yourself. Instead of saying no, paring down, and embracing quality of life over quantity of commitments, you allowed your life to spin out of control. And it's left you without half a second to take a deep breath.

Take a minute. A long minute even.

Breathe in.

Breathe out.

Our society glorifies busyness and champions the adrenaline rush. *If we're not going fast*, they say, *we're not moving forward.* On top of this, women often have the habit of stepping into the role of martyr, sacrificing ourselves for the "greater good." We believe we're doing the selfless thing, but we eventually self-sabotage by not investing time in ourselves. My dad calls this a "crash-and-burn."

Have you ever wondered why flight attendants tell travelers that if oxygen masks deploy, you should secure yours before helping your kids or anyone else? They give this instruction because if you can't breathe, there's no way you can help anyone else. The same goes for day-to-day life. You may be bending over backward to give your children a good life, but if you're not taking care of yourself too, you're moving backward—away from that goal.

YOU CAN'T DRAW WATER FROM AN EMPTY WELL

On a busy day, I took my stance in our driveway, preparing to lift all 150 pounds of our gentle giant bullmastiff into the back of my car. Briggs was a young seven years old, but his limbs were weak. He knew the routine, and he placed his front right paw onto the back bumper of my Explorer. Brady waited quietly in his car seat, watching our struggle. I placed my hands under Briggs's front left paw and lifted it onto the bumper. Briggs scooted closer to the car while I bear-hugged his back legs and lifted him onto the folded-down backseat, which was now broken from his weight after multiple trips to the vet. He circled as best he could in the small space and slowly settled into the car, laying his head on his paws. He was a sweet, sweet pup—an absolute dream with children. I rubbed the big wrinkles on his face, and he closed his eyes, ready for the fifteen-minute ride.

When we arrived at the animal hospital for Briggs's chemotherapy appointment, Brady slipped his hand into mine, and I took hold of Briggs's blue leash. We sat on the steps waiting for the train to go by, as it always did at this time each Friday. I saw Brady's eyes light up as he sat next to Briggs, one hand on the dog's back and the other waving frantically at the conductor. What a joyful spot in the middle of our difficult visit. We walked inside and hugged Briggs before our vet, perhaps the kindest veterinarian in the world, took him back for his treatment. When Briggs was diagnosed with lymphoma, we'd made the choice to pursue treatment to improve his quality of life for the time he had left with us.

As his appointments continued to mount, I moved into what I call Captain Mode. I knew I could manage the difficult situation we were in. I could make this easier on everyone. In the spring, shortly after we began treatment on Briggs, Bryan's father was diagnosed with cancer and passed away suddenly—only seventeen short days later. To say it was a difficult time for our little family would be a gross understatement. I saw my husband in tears for the first time in the five years we'd been together. I saw Brady experience the sadness of death and answered big questions about heaven and sickness and why bad things happen to good people (and good pups).

Still, I worked in Captain Mode, trying to be the glue that held everyone together. I decided to take hold of our crazy life and fix it. For any problems we had, I was determined to find solutions.

> *Captain Mode:*
> *I've got this.*
> *I can do this*
> *alone. I will save*
> *the day and*
> *steer the ship.*

We'd been in the middle of exhausting fertility treatments, so we decided to take it up a notch and pursue more aggressive options. I'd been considering a big production change with our Simplified Planners, so I pursued it. Grief and sadness mounted at home. Fertility treatments weren't working. Briggs was getting sicker. The pain of losing Bryan's dad was real and raw. Work was busier than ever. Without extended family nearby, I found myself taking on more and more to help our family get back to normal and be happy again. I put all my hope and trust in my own two hands. Does anyone see a crash-and-burn coming? I wish I would have.

I skipped meals, lost sleep, and worked harder than ever

before as we mourned Bryan's dad and our sweet Briggs lost his battle with cancer. It was painful for all of us. I powered through with the help of caffeine and a burning goal to simply get to the other side. I was determined. *If I work hard enough at keeping it all together,* I thought, *we'll get there.*

One late summer evening, I sat on my bed looking down the hall at Bryan playing with Brady on the floor. My parents had traveled down from Pensacola to come to our rescue and help with the accumulating housework. I had left the house to them for a moment to catch my breath by myself.

I sat there in a mess of tears, overwhelmed by how much I loved our little family and desperate for something more to give them. Our life was in chaos, and as we dealt with sickness and sadness, the laundry, cleaning, and grocery shopping had fallen by the wayside. I couldn't find peace in our house because it was a disaster. And I was riddled with worry over what awful thing would happen next. I sat with my legs crossed and rubbed my hands on my feet anxiously. Oddly, the side of my right foot felt completely numb.

I ran my fingers over the bottom of my foot and felt pressure but no sensation. My anxiety grew as I instinctively reached for my phone and began to Google my symptom. The Internet spat back a list of terminal diseases and terrible diagnoses that could explain why my foot was numb. Terrified, I walked around my room, hoping to stomp it out or make it go away. When I realized it wasn't changing, I walked to the living room to tell Bryan. He shrugged it off and told me it would go away. I told my mom and dad, hoping they'd know some simple explanation, but no one seemed as worried as I was.

When I woke the next morning and found that my foot was still numb, I made an immediate appointment with my doctor. He found my symptom puzzling and ordered a battery of tests. Over the next few weeks of blood tests and doctor appointments, I felt a fear like I've never known. At every stoplight, after every e-mail, and in the moments before I fell asleep every night, I searched the Internet for answers. All sorts of things could cause intense headaches, vision problems, weight loss, heart palpitations, numbness, and muscle twitches. Finally my doctor referred me to a well-known neurologist, and the next thing I knew, I was strapped down with Velcro and being pushed into a cold, white MRI machine for brain scans.

As the scanner made its signature banging sounds, I silently prayed and cried, eyes squeezed shut. I prayed for my health and for my family. I wanted more than anything to go back to February—to Brady's Elmo party, where we celebrated his second birthday—before the hard stuff flipped our normal life on its head. The technologist told me through the microphone that I had one more minute left. I still hadn't opened my eyes while inside the machine. But as she rolled me out, I knew that whatever was wrong with me was recorded in black-and-white images. We'd soon have some answers. I finally felt a slight lift in the weight on my shoulders for the first time in months.

Five days later, I sat in the neurologist's office. I hadn't worn makeup that day for fear of the news I might be given. (Who wants a bad diagnosis *and* streaks, right?) My palms were sweaty, and worry coursed through my veins. He came in and sat down and slowly read through my chart. I studied his face, searching for any sign of concern—some sort of answer to my issues. He put the manila folder down and took off his glasses as he turned to face me.

"You're perfectly healthy, Emily," he said. I sat back, almost dizzy from the way every muscle in my body let go of an indescribable amount of tension. Overwhelmed and confused, I let tears fall down my cheeks.

"I don't understand," I said. I repeated all my symptoms while he smiled sympathetically and nodded his head.

"You are running yourself into the ground, Emily," he gently said. "Each of your symptoms is being caused by intense stress on your body. You have to slow down, or you're going to end up with something much worse than a numb foot. You're going to kill yourself."

I walked to my car that afternoon somewhat in shock. How had I allowed myself to get to this awful place? How was I going to dig myself out? I'd love to tell you that this knowledge gave me permission to immediately relax and that life was wonderful from that moment on. But I'd stolen the wheel from God while trying to steer our family out of the grieving process toward a happier story, and I'd driven myself straight into a wall. Head on. Crash-and-burn. While the answer felt like a sudden smack in the face, it was an obvious diagnosis. I'd made taking care of myself my last priority. It was going to take some time to bounce back from this one. I determined that recovery from that summer meant saying no, letting go, and learning to take care of myself and let God handle the rest.

After that summer of 2013, I took my doctor's advice and started to fill my heart and mind and body with goodness: healthy food, water, rest, and truth. I had driven myself too close to the edge. I hadn't realized that worry, anxiety, the need for control, and the chase of perfection zap the life, energy, and health from our bodies. I learned *so* much from the terrible summer of 2013. My experience taught me that when we are desperately worried, we often point our focus inward, robbing us of faith and weakening our hearts. When we are weak, we aren't our best selves. We can't draw water from an empty well. And when we are empty, we're good for no one.

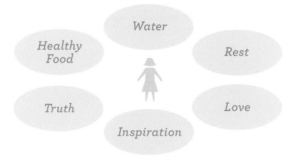

You may be thinking, *I'm in it, Emily. How do I get out? I'm right where you were, or I'm surely on my way there.* My answer for you is this: give yourself permission to slow down. In fact, give yourself permission to just stop. Press pause on as much as possible, and take inventory of your life. What are your commitments and responsibilities? What can go? What are your priorities? What can you say no to?

LIFE INVENTORY: *What are you missing? What makes you feel deeply alive? And how can you fill your heart up with that, even if just a tiny bit?*

I love the beach. I love the way I can see God's handiwork in the ocean. I love the freedom of the salt air, open shore, and sand beneath my feet. I love how messy I feel at the beach. It's just one of the things that makes me feel alive. Then there's strong coffee. Summer sunsets on my front porch in our white rocking chairs with my husband. I love having my entire family together. I love laughing with them and the way they speak life into me. I love being a mother. I love rocking sleeping babies and the way Tyler plays with my gold necklace—his favorite toy on this earth. I love the way Brady tells knock-knock jokes and always forgets the punch line. I love Caroline's smile (those lips!)

Give yourself **PERMISSION** *to slow down.*

and her infectious laugh that makes every fiber of my being smile. I love white, open spaces and art and creative people and old books and history and fancy dresses and swatch books. I love stripes, the gospel, acoustic guitars, my mama's blueberry pound cake, and the way she takes care of our family. I love honest conversation with my dad and the way he loves endlessly. I love writing and singing (though I'm terrible at it). I love country music. I love people.

♥ *I love . . .*

_____

_____

_____

_____

_____

Why, oh why, am I not I filling my free time with all these things? Instead of Facebook. Or Instagram. Or another episode of *Parenthood*. Or wiping the counters for the fifteenth time. Our wells could be brimming with more of the good stuff. Imagine the refreshing, life-giving water that well could provide to those around you. With that overflow, imagine how you could love others in the same way you have shown love to yourself!

What would your life look like if you let your well be filled, even five minutes a day, with the things that make you feel deeply alive? It's not as hard as it seems to infuse your life with tiny moments of joy that will soon add up to a spiritual shift. Wake up twenty minutes early to savor your favorite dark-roast coffee with hazelnut cream. Put pictures of your last beach trip on your desk. Ditch the dirty kitchen counter tonight for five minutes of rocking-chair time with your little one. Invest in yourself. You get out what you put in.

You get **OUT** *what you put* **IN**.

Chapter 3

PLANNING AND SIMPLICITY

Outer order contributes to inner calm.

GRETCHEN RUBIN

WE'RE ALL CHASING JOY. Some joy comes when you least expect it. And some joy comes because you set yourself up for it. As a family, we have made specific choices to create that joy. For instance, we signed Brady up for soccer, knowing that even if he never scored a goal, he'd find joy in playing on a team, being encouraged by his coach, and learning a new skill. Every Saturday when we leave the soccer field, he's so proud of himself. (I'm not even sure he knows whether his team won or lost.) That brings Bryan and me big joy.

Personally, I find joy in a tidy home. I find happiness in the calmness and confidence of knowing I'm prepared for the week ahead on a Sunday evening. Lunches are made. The fridge is stocked. Laundry is folded and put away. Our schedules are synced, and we're ready for a good Monday. Granted, not every Sunday ends that way. But when one does, I feel like I have space to breathe, to enjoy the small stuff, and to spend my week doing what family loves.

So how do we tactically set ourselves up for joy? It starts with grace, continues with a plan, and ends with grace. When you make a plan, wrap it up in a giant hug of grace, because it may not happen, or it may not happen the way you intended. Let go of the perfect plan, and pursue a good and flexible plan—one that will give you the freedom to go with the flow and find the joy hidden in the in-between moments. Let's explore the tactical steps involved with setting yourself up for joy. You can put specific systems in place to bring a little more order to your everyday circus.

In this chapter, we're going to dive into three such systems: one to organize your time, one to organize your belongings, and one to organize your home. Automating these things can free up an awful lot of brain space for life to happen—and more importantly, for other people to fill up your heart.

A SYSTEM FOR YOUR TIME: SUNDAY PREP

Aren't Sundays wonderful? God gave us Sundays to rest and recharge for the week ahead. For me, that means spending my afternoon preparing my family and home for the next six days, then filling my own tank with the good stuff so I can be the best wife, mom, and businesswoman possible. When I designed the Simplified Planner, I included the Weekly Prep checklist on every Sunday space because I really believe it makes a giant difference in our productivity, our peace of mind, and the pace at which we operate during the week. But even more than that, I believe these four tasks carve space for the stuff that matters most—dinnertime conversations, evening walks in the neighborhood, and actual face time with the people we love.

1: *Plan Meals for the Week Ahead*

I don't know about you, but the people at my house expect me to feed them every single day. (What's with that?!) My husband works pretty late and has a long commute, so I'm the meal planner and executive chef in our house—which means I'm really great at working the slow cooker and ordering take-out. It's an endless cycle—we're talking about the next meal before the dishes are even washed. What gives?

My parents had dinner on the table at the same time every day of my childhood. And they made it look pretty effortless. Looking back, I realize now that my mom actually had quite a system in place to make dinnertime run smoothly. Honestly, she set the bar for being organized and showed me how a little preparation could change an entire week.

She wrote weeknight dinners on a monthly calendar taped to the fridge. These recipes were pulled from a little book of family favorites that she always kept in rotation. Each week, she used that calendar to make a grocery list. Then she and my dad did the shopping on Sunday mornings. She looked at her calendar every evening to prepare whatever she could for the next day's dinner. When we all got home from work and school, she and my dad made dinner, and we all sat around the table to talk about our days. It happened like that every single day, and dinnertime was a really special time for all of us to connect over a good meal.

When I started making dinner for my little family, I didn't

have a plan, but I really wanted to create the same special daily experience. Things went a little bit like this: Emily walks into the kitchen at 5:30 after work and throws her purse on the counter. Emily opens the fridge to see four eggs, an outdated carton of milk, three stalks of celery, and half a jar of salsa. She remembers the frozen chicken breasts but realizes it's too late to thaw them. Emily feels frustrated and hungry and frantically throws something together.

Fast-forward a few years later. With a little more experience under my belt and my mom's good advice, I follow her technique and set myself up for dinnertime success. Remember the idea of wrapping your plan in a grace hug? Well, we eat a lot of takeout and pizza on the floor (a really fun tradition for our family), and it totally works for us. I'm not the best cook, and I'm fine with that. We have three kids under five and two demanding jobs. I give myself grace and permission to not be Supermom in the kitchen. It's just not my gift.

> *Don't sacrifice the good to chase the perfect.*

Pizza on the floor on Fridays is delicious and fun and totally okay. Paper plates, napkins, and delivery from our favorite local spot (in just thirty minutes!) means happy kids, full bellies, and not-stressed-out Mom and Dad. Plus, cleanup is a breeze. The lesson here? Don't sacrifice the good to chase the perfect. A slight modification of an old proverb applies here: an ounce of preparation is worth a pound of happiness. And plan B isn't always second best. I always try to remember that eating delivery pizza together on the floor is better than eating a well-prepared seven-course dinner alone.

For those plan-A nights when you need to whip up some nourishment for yourself and your loved ones, having a plan is key. It will keep you from wasting energy with scrambling, making frantic decisions, and throwing less-than-delicious things together at the last minute.

SUNDAY MEAL-PLANNING

1. Make a list of ten to twenty easy dinners.
2. Write them out on a monthly calendar.
3. Put that calendar on your fridge for easy reference and planning.
4. Make your grocery lists ahead of time, and choose a time to stock up.

2: Tidy Up for a Clean Slate

I used to think it was so strange that my mom wiped the water droplets from the inside of the kitchen sink every night before she went to bed. *Doesn't water belong in a sink?* I thought. *Isn't it just going to get wet again the next time it's used?* I didn't understand her odd nightly ritual until I had my own house. After cleaning the kitchen, I'd marvel at how shiny and clean the sink was and found myself doing the same thing after dinner every night. The next morning, I'd wake up to a clean, shiny kitchen and start my day with just a little bit of peace. Mom wasn't wiping out the sink just to keep it clean. She was doing it because it felt good to walk into a clean kitchen in the morning. She was setting herself up for that peace. And that peace brought her joy.

I follow her example in my own house on Sunday afternoons. I grab a laundry basket and walk from room to room grabbing anything that feels out of place. Shoes, papers, trash, cups, laundry—they all go into the basket. Sometimes it takes two baskets. But when I leave each room, it is on its way to being clean. I dump the basket in my living room and sort each item by where it goes: trash can, laundry room, bedroom, or elsewhere. Bryan and I put the piles away, and *voilà*! With a few pairs of hands, what could have taken hours upon hours has taken thirty minutes.

Then Monday morning, when I walk into the living room, I'm able to breathe. I'm not immediately bombarded with tasks: picking up toys, putting laundry in the laundry room, putting dishes in the dishwasher. Instead, I'm able to make my cup of coffee and sit for five minutes taking in the morning before the kids wake up.

The way you begin your day sets the stage for the rest of your day. Here comes the grace hug though: on some days I go to bed with dirty dishes in the sink, toys everywhere, and papers scattered across my kitchen counters. And you know what? That's okay. Sometimes there's a bigger priority—a friend who needs a late-night helping hand or other work to be done or a child to cuddle—and the straightening up can wait. Carving out fifteen minutes when possible to prepare your space makes a world of difference.

SUNDAY TIDY-UP

1. Grab a laundry basket.
2. Gather everything that is out of place in every room.
3. Sort the stuff in the basket by room it belongs in.
4. Put it away.
5. Wipe the countertops and sweep the floors.
6. Light a candle. It always makes a room feel fresher.

3: Write Out a Plan for the Week

This may sound obvious coming from someone who owns a day planner company. But trust me. I started this business and created the Simplified Planner because I get what it feels like to have a million things going on. There is so much to manage, and there are so many things to balance. At some point I realized I have a limited capacity to hold information in my brain, and I needed a place to put it all. Enter the Simplified Planner.

Bryan and I have developed a ritual around writing things out. Every Sunday, we compare schedules for the week. I make note in my planner if he won't be home for dinner one night or if I have an early-morning meeting and need him to take Brady to school. We sync our schedules and make a plan for the week. I look over the next six days to see if there's anything special I need to add to the grocery list for school activities or playdates.

This sounds like a super obvious solution, but how many times have you found yourself surprised by something during the week when you knew in the back of your head it was coming? Looking ahead helps everyone in the family know his or her responsibilities. It helps us flow with whatever the week will throw at us with a little more flexibility and preparedness. Taking just a few minutes to invest in this step will save hours of stress and relieve that nagging feeling that you're forgetting something throughout the course of the week.

SUNDAY PLANNING

1. Set a weekly tradition to meet with your family to compare schedules.
2. Mark any times anyone will not be home for dinner.
3. Mark reminders for yourself for any events you need to prepare for.

4: Fill Your Tank

I'm going to say it again (and again and again, mostly to remind myself): you're good for no one when you're running on empty. Take care of yourself. Take half an hour after dinner to read a good book. Let your mind wander. Do something messy with your kids. Indulge in a good coffee dessert with your girl-friends. Soak in God's Word and sing loud at church. By the time you get to this step, you've probably prepped everyone in your family for the week ahead. Don't forget to take care of yourself too. Take a long shower. Wash your hair. Paint your nails. Do the little things you may not have time for during the week.

I don't know about you, but I feel like a million bucks when my hair is straightened and my nails are painted a pretty color. And feeling just a little more put-together allows me to stand a little taller and tackle the week a little better. That's right: I just told you painted nails are the secret to everything! Of course I'm kidding, but small things do add up. Identify what those things are for you. Do you feel great after exercising? Give yourself time for a long run on Sunday afternoon. Do you love a good book? Read a book in the bathtub! Do you love cooking? Make a really delicious meal for Sunday evenings. See what I did there? I paired a feel-good activity with a to-do activity. A two-in-one task, if you will. Those are the best ones to check off because they give us a sense of accomplishment along with a little relaxation.

SUNDAY REST

1. Carve time for yourself in the evening—at least thirty minutes.
2. Turn off the screens, and turn on some music that inspires you and settles your soul.

3. Dig in to whatever makes you happiest and sets you up for success in the morning. Prepare yourself emotionally for a great Monday.

A SYSTEM FOR YOUR STUFF: PARING DOWN

Now that you've carved out time for prep work, let's turn to your stuff. Organizing is a big job with a lot of pay-off. Think about the way you feel when your home is tidy. The kitchen is clean. The dishwasher is empty. The laundry is folded and put away. The toys are in the baskets. The shoes are all in line. There's something so good about that atmosphere. I can tackle the world when my home is in order. You know why that feeling is so hard to achieve? Two reasons: (1) some of us have crazy little ones running around, tearing it all apart all day long, and (2) we just have too much stuff. Our homes feel messy and cluttered because we have too many things taking up space, out of place, and requiring our attention—ultimately distracting us from what matters.

Sometimes the problem isn't our lack of organizational solutions; it's our abundance of things.

How many times have you purchased the cool organizers and the fancy systems and products to arrange all your things? If you have sixteen pairs of flip-flops, a fancy shoe rack will make your flip-flops pretty and all in a row, but it's not going to change the fact that you have *sixteen pairs of flip-flops*. Sometimes the problem isn't our lack of organizational solutions; it's our abundance of things. There are three types of "things":

1. **Things we need:** our pillow, the pair of jeans we wear three times a week, and lightbulbs.
2. **Things we want to keep:** our children's baby books, heirlooms from our grandmothers, and family recipes.
3. **Things that take up space:** hangers from the dry cleaners, T-shirts we don't like to wear, and fancy dishes we never use.

We all have these three types of things in our homes. The question is, what do we do with them? Here's the goal: keep all the things we need, treasure the things we want to keep, and discard or donate the things that are taking up space. We can put a system in place to simplify our physical space in a way that makes us productive, frees us from constant straightening up, and allows us more mental and physical white space. Now let's look at how to handle each type of "thing."

1. Things We Need

We all need things like cups, shoes, and laundry detergent. But do you really need *all* those T-shirts? How many of those cups do you actually drink out of? Is anything gained from having four different bottles of detergent? Begin separating the things you need from the things you don't, starting with two trash bags: one for donations and one to throw out or recycle. (Beware: you may need many of these bags as you move through your house.) I find it easiest to go room by room, selecting items to trash or donate and placing those items into the appropriate bag. When a bag is full, place it by your front door to remind you to do something with it.

As you make your decision for each item, remember this: when in doubt, say goodbye. Free yourself from whatever it is and move on. If you have unnecessary multiples of certain items—nail clippers, pencil sharpeners, or black swimsuits, for example—choose the best or your favorite, and toss or donate the rest. You may find yourself with empty drawers or odd open space. Resist the urge to fill it with something! Allow that space to be margin for what matters: your family, your work, your treasures.

THE BAG PLAN

- Master bathroom
- Master closet
- Master bedroom
- Kitchen
- Living room
- Other living spaces

2. Things We Want to Keep

I used to keep a very old recipe tin tucked away in my pantry. Inside it are about sixty handwritten recipes from my grandmother. She was one of the most special people in my life. Even seeing her handwriting fills my heart with love for the beautiful woman she was and the way she taught me about faith. When I see that little tin container, I remember the way she used to hug me tight and say, "You are so sweet, my Emily Sue." It makes me smile even writing that.

Recently I moved the tin out of my pantry and placed it where there used to be a ceramic vase full of fake flowers. Every time I walk past that recipe tin, I smile. Want to know how I felt walking past my ceramic vase of fake flowers? Blank. Nothing. How nice it is to move something I want to keep—something I treasure—where it fills me with happiness that otherwise wasn't there. It may not match my décor as nicely as the fake tulips, but it sure fills my well with something special.

I encourage you to identify the special things in your life, and for each one, get rid of something you're not using. For instance, those scrapbooks tucked into drawers and closets could replace the coffee-table books you've never read (or intend to read). Imagine the happiness you'll experience flipping through them after dinner in the evenings. Put the special things you own in a place where you can see and appreciate them.

MY THOUGHTS

Which items that you own mean a lot to you?

What would be a more visible location for them?

No. 1

No. 2

No. 3

3. Things That Take Up Space

You know what these things are. You may have come across them when you were figuring out the things you need. Now go back and look again, trash bags in hand. I encourage you to be relentless with this task. Again, when in doubt, say goodbye. Do you have bins of old baby toys that you're not going to use again? Donate them. Imagine how much fun those toys will be for another child. Clothes you're going to wear when you "lose that baby weight"? Donate them. Free yourself from feeling that you aren't thin enough or good enough every time you look at them. Make room. Clear space. Say goodbye.

> *Physical clutter is mental clutter.*

Trust me—the freedom you'll have when you rid your physical space of clutter is priceless. It equals mental space in more ways than you'll ever realize.

Determining where your belongings fall in these categories will help ensure that your stuff doesn't crowd your life—that it works for you, not against you. So reclaim the moments you spend dusting or arranging unnecessary things, and replace them with moments that make your life richer, better, and more connected to those around you.

A SYSTEM FOR YOUR ENVIRONMENT: SPACE FOR YOUR LIFE

Once you've decluttered and purged the unnecessary from your home, it's time to make your space work for you. You deserve a home that fulfills some basic functions: serves as a place of comfort, holds décor that fills your well as you walk past it, and equips you to be your best. We used to keep Brady's shoes upstairs in his bedroom (seems like an obvious place for them, right?). But every morning, he'd come downstairs dressed but carrying his shoes because he's not quite old enough to tie them himself. Then every afternoon, he'd take them off downstairs, and we'd have to truck them upstairs. Finally I realized we were making a lot of extra trips up and down the stairs for this. So we set up an old basket near our front door. All his shoes live there now. And every day they go back to that place.

When you're figuring out what works best in your home, try this trick. Keep notes on your phone, and add to them as you go about a normal day. What could be moved or changed to help you manage life better? Where are you expending energy that you could be saving? Are you the mom who always forgets to put the water bottle in your kid's lunchbox? (Because if you are, I feel you, mama!) The mornings are crazy and hectic—no wonder you don't have brain space for that water bottle. Don't be ashamed to put a sticky note on the front door or do whatever it takes to make your life flow.

Always wasting time looking for keys? Maybe it's time to break out that gorgeous bowl you got for your wedding or invest in a cute key rack. Bills, receipts, and little papers floating around everywhere? Try a shoe box placed strategically where most of them end up (with a commitment to emptying it on a certain day each week or month). Technology scattered all over the house? Try keeping your cords plugged into the same place, and line those soldiers up at night to recharge. It doesn't matter if it doesn't look cute. You can take time and figure that out later. The goal here is function. You don't need the Pinterest-perfect home; you need a home that works for you and makes you feel alive. You need a space, fancy or not, that allows you to be your best self.

SAMPLE HOUSE-FLOW NOTES

Tackling junk drawers

- More than likely, the issue with your junk drawer is that you have too many things in it. How much of that drawer do you actually use? I bet it's close to 15 percent. Seriously. I know that's how my junk drawer works! If you don't use it, toss it.
- Keep like items in the same place. Nail files belong in the bathroom, not in your junk drawer because you think you might

need to use them in that very location one day. Playing cards belong with board games.

- Dump the drawer and put the necessities back in. Don't try to organize a full drawer. Start with a clean slate.

Mastering drop spots (places where your family members drop and leave things)

- Keep only the items you use on a daily basis out in plain view. Tuck coats, tote bags, and handbags away in a closet for the next time you'll need them.
- If you keep shoes by your front door, put them in a box or basket. Trust me, I wasted years of my life shuffling shoes up and down the stairs from their spot at the front door to their home in my kids' closets. A box or basket is an easy trick.
- Place a shoe box where your family members regularly drop keys, receipts, and cell phones. A catch-all will go a long way toward getting junk out of view.

Creating happy places

- Fill your nightstand with items you use before and after you sleep—*and nothing else*. Move all that nail polish to the bathroom. In your nightstand, be sure you have lip balm, a notepad, a pen, tissues, your current favorite read, or any other necessity. Give everything else a proper home.
- Allow your workspace, your bathtub, or whatever spot is your

retreat to be a true place of inspiration and relaxation. Move a candle to that area. Stack your favorite books nearby. Make the space work for you.

- Replace old artwork with photographs. Display special mementos or heirlooms. Remember, your home and the happiest places within it are not showrooms. Mess is okay! Personal décor can be so special and meaningful. Being comfortable is key.

Our physical space has an enormous impact on our happiness. The things we fill our home with can either distract us or inspire us. By devoting some attention to organizing our time, our stuff, and our environment, we can make room for that happiness and inspiration. Your happiness by no means *depends* on things being clean and tidy. Thinking that way is like hopping a fast train to Anxietyville, and it's just plain not real life (we'll talk about that in the next chapter). But remember: you are in charge of your space, and your space is a tool. You can wield that tool to your advantage.

So take a day like Sunday to give yourself a clean slate. Choose to be inspired by saying goodbye to the objects that are taking up space, moving the things you treasure into sight, and playing favorites with the things you need. Donate or discard the stuff that is taking up valuable real estate—both in your home and in your heart. And vigilantly look for ways to improve the function of your space. It's a simple game of yes or no that can have a significant effect on your day-to-day life.

You don't need a Pinterest-perfect home; you need a home that works for you and makes you feel **ALIVE**.

Chapter 4

MARGIN FOR WHAT MATTERS

*The battle for our hearts are [sic] fought
on the pages of our calendars.*

BOB GOFF

IF YOU'RE LIKE ME, you feel the battle in your heart when
you look at your calendar, as Bob Goff so wisely put it. What
we spend our time on so often indicates what we value. But so
many of us have the same calendar problem: when we squeeze
appointment after meeting after errand onto our schedules,
we edge out time for joy. We tell the savorable moments of
joy, "I just don't have time for you. But I sure do have time for
committees and Facebook and folding clothes."

I used to find that my days were pretty well organized. I could
tackle what I needed to do in the time I had. But somewhere
along the way, I decided that I needed the adrenaline rush of

back-to-back appointments and extra responsibilities. Besides, I wasn't a good mom/wife/friend/daughter/professional if I didn't pack my calendar to maximum capacity. Right? Between laundry and work and someone needing his or her shoes tied, my days were crammed full. From sunrise to sunset, I was full-speed ahead—eating in the car, checking my e-mail every ten minutes, playing with the kids, and multitasking like a pro.

Sound familiar? Instead of prioritizing our commitments and carefully choosing what we fill our time with, we so often focus on just making life happen—on surviving—every day. Though we all desperately want to slow down and make time for what matters, we don't give ourselves permission to reevaluate. Just imagine what we're missing out on when we put our heads down and barrel through the day.

MAX CAPACITY

This may come as good news to you: *you have a maximum capacity.* There is a concrete limit to how much you can fit in your brain and how much your body can handle. At some point, when there is too much for you to remember or worry about or think through, you start to forget things. Tasks fall through the cracks. Appointments are forgotten. And slowly you find yourself in the middle of a giant mess. This is what happens when we're overwhelmed, overbooked, overcommitted, and overstressed.

MY THOUGHTS

Things I'd rather be doing than _____.

No. 1

No. 2

No. 3

Take a look at
your **CALENDAR.**
What commitments are not
absolutely essential to the function of your
family? What commitments steal margin from
your days instead of bringing value to them?

A common reaction to this is to feel guilty, or like you're not as sharp as you used to be, or like you're failing in some way. Not so! This is simple cause and effect: you have limits, and you have them for a reason. And friend, you do not have to drive yourself like a beast of burden to go beyond your capacity.

So what do you do to stop the insane cycle? The only way to lighten an overfull plate is to take things off it—to quit things, to say no, to uncommit. Do you begrudgingly serve on a committee that you don't enjoy but stick with because "it will look good on your résumé"? Quit! Is your child overcommitted with extracurricular activities because everyone else is? Say no! We're all looking for someone to give us permission to slow down—to be perfectly imperfect and uniquely different. So here it is. You have permission. I don't want you in the doctor's office with palpitations and a numb foot like I was. Make margin for what matters. This is your one precious, crazy life. White space in your calendar is priceless. Why work so hard to fill it up? Aren't the in-between moments where we find the most joy?

THE GOOD STUFF OF LIFE

Before I started my company, I worked as a development manager for a large hospice in Pensacola, Florida. Though I worked in the fun, fast-paced, world of fundraising and events, I learned daily about the often difficult end-of-life services our organization offered its patients and their families. Time after time, I heard stories of patients sharing memories, wishes, and regrets during their last few days. The stories were sobering and beautiful at the same time. Never did patients mention how glad they were that they worked late every day. Or how proud they were of the money in their bank account. Not once did they mention how fulfilled they felt at the number of followers they had on social media or how many achievements they'd racked up in their lifetime. Instead they spoke fondly of once-in-a-lifetime love, family, and adventure. They spoke about the raw, real, good stuff of life.

In their final moments, these people talked about big family dinners and long-awaited reconciliations with old friends. They spoke deeply sincere, heartfelt words of love and life into the hearts of their family members—sentiments they wished they'd shared years ago. They spent their final days marveling over the good stuff, the memories made in the margin—not their biggest accomplishments. These stories gave me a new perspective on life, one of gratitude and immediacy. When our time becomes short, our priorities are suddenly jolted into place. I don't know about you, but this makes some of what I fill my days with seem very trivial and unimportant.

What if we lived every day with that perspective? What if we were unapologetic about our priorities in a genuine, heartfelt way? What if we poured love onto people and spoke truth and encouragement without concern about their response?

We don't have to wait until the end of life. Right this moment, we can construct our schedules in a way that allows us to truly savor the good stuff in between the have-tos of life. We can choose long dinners with people we love, meaningful conversations that stir our souls, baby giggles and hand-holding and slow walks through beautiful places. What would happen if we intentionally carved out white space for these memories instead of allowing ourselves to be busy for busyness's sake?

This battle has been a difficult one for me, but I'm happy to say there's hope on the other side. For years, I've struggled to find ways to make the good stuff the priority and let the extra commitments happen as they may, rather than the other way around. Making margin in our days means clearing room in our schedule to slow down, but it also means choosing to be still even when tasks need to be completed. The magic is that when I think about extra commitments as secondary to the good stuff, tasks start to fall away naturally and people become the most important. The have-tos are still important, but they're less of a nuisance. Emptying the dishwasher means gathering clean dishes for a family dinner. Folding laundry means rejoicing in the tiny baby clothes for the

What would you do in the white space of your days? Where would you be still, and which moments would you savor?

tiny babies we prayed so long and hard for. For me, this enormous heart-change was born out of very tactical steps: being intentionally still, definitively choosing the good over the perfect, and fiercely guarding the pages of my calendar.

BE STILL

I've been a pretty high-energy, ambitious project person since I was a little girl. I'd search for project after project to

> "BE STILL,
> AND KNOW
> THAT I
> AM GOD."
> —PSALM 46:10

throw myself into. My idea of a great time was to start with an idea, create something with my hands, and follow it through to the end. I made lemonade stands in my driveway and elaborate Barbie mansions out of my mom's old perfume boxes. I put on plays with my cousins (complete with refreshments and playbills). Throughout my childhood and young adulthood, I was full-speed ahead all the time, working and worrying, trying, creating, and adventuring. My grandmother used to tell me, "Emily, just be still" (referring to Psalm 46:10—and also literally telling me to *slow down*, probably for fear that I'd knock something over).

My grandmother's real message didn't sink in until I was older, when I realized that I have a tendency to make myself busy, run on adrenaline, and miss the in-between moments of quiet. After my crash-and-burn doctor's office revelation, I began to give myself permission to give in to the mess. When life became overwhelming, I threw my hands in the air (literally at times) and let the good stuff win. When juggling work *and* motherhood became too much, I took time off or put the laptop away to stomp in mud puddles outside with my children. When laundry mounted and housework screamed my name, I left the madness behind and went to the park for a picnic instead. Sometimes, the way to step off the hamster wheel is to literally step away from the stressor. I began to learn that in those messy moments, I felt like my realest self. I wasn't hustling to make something happen. Instead I was just being still and drinking in the moments—choosing the good life.

A few days ago, I sat in a chair at our big wooden kitchen table. Beneath me was a sea of dropped Cheerios. Our twins, Tyler and Caroline, giggled and squirmed in their high chairs, pawing at a few Cheerios on their trays. I studied Tyler while he laid his chubby hand on a Cheerio, closed four of his fingers, and stuck his thumb in his mouth. He wiggled his four fingers until the Cheerio worked itself into his mouth beside his thumb. *Nice technique.* I giggled. We call him Pooh Bear sometimes because he's just so squishy and easy and sweet as honey. He smiled at his accomplishment and reached for another one.

I looked slowly around the room at the mess in my kitchen and stopped my gaze at Caroline. Though she and Tyler are the same age, they are very different. We like to say she's spicy. She has personality for days and the most beautiful puckered lips you ever did see. Instead of calmly eating her Cheerios, she banged on her tray to make them bounce. On my other side, Brady concentrated intensely, coloring a peacock four shades of green. I watched the way his little fingers gripped the crayon and his eyes moved back and forth from the page to his crayon box, carefully considering his next color choice.

I made margin that day by choosing not to immediately clean up the kitchen. Instead, I savored a few rare, quiet moments with my little ones and let the mess wait. That's a hard choice for someone like me. I am constantly picking up, confident that a clean house equals a happy home. But so often, that's not the case. I'm slowly learning that my happiest, most special moments happen when the circus is at its peak.

CHOOSING THE GOOD OVER THE PERFECT

Our kitchen counters may not be spotless, but the drips of ice cream came from an impromptu late-night sundae party, so I'll happily wipe them up.

My shirt may be wrinkled when I walk into the preschool classroom, but that's because we had a tickle fight on the couch before we left.

We may not have been on a fancy date in three years, but

we've enjoyed many a good conversation on the front porch, holding hands and a baby monitor at the same time.

I'm not good at baking beautifully decorated cookies for a birthday party, but I'm really good at thinking them up and ordering them from people who are (and that's a talent in and of itself, right?).

Our floors may be covered with Cheerios, but the mess is worth being able to savor the way my baby wiggles the Cheerios into his mouth with all five fingers.

We might be scrambling to get out the door every morning because of three little bodies to dress and feed, but on some days we worried we'd never have even one squirmy little love, so I'll savor the scramble.

My hands may be dirty, but I sat for hours in the yard digging tunnels in the dirt, carving roads for Brady's trucks, and pointing out all the bugs and leaves and treasures we discovered along the way.

Life may be messy, but the mess is worth it.

A PLANNER WON'T CHANGE YOUR LIFE

You read that right. I'm telling you that a planner won't change your life, even though I'm a "planner maker," as Brady would say. The fact is, I created the Simplified Planner because I was an overwhelmed new mom desperate for some simplicity and structure. The battle for my heart was being lost on the pages of my calendar! Much like every woman I knew, I had added commitments and appointments to my calendar until it'd reached its limit. I searched high and low for some cure-all to organize all the crazy things I had going on. I tried all sorts of complicated systems and fancy agendas, hoping that somewhere in the ingenuity of all these newfangled products I'd find a solution to my problem. It took a few crash-and-burn experiences for me to realize that it simply didn't exist. No system was going to magically make my life easier and give me more time to spend with my family.

Much like a closet overflowing with sixteen pairs of flip-flops, my schedule had a clutter issue. I hadn't sorted out what mattered and what I needed versus what was just taking up space. It wasn't until I sat down with a big piece of paper and decided what I was going to say yes to and what I was going to say no to that I was able to trim the fat from my life. I gave a loud and enthusiastic yes to my family, my people, and adventure. I said no to being constantly connected to e-mail and my phone, constantly cleaning my house, and extra obligatory commitments that didn't serve the people I loved.

Once I got my priorities in line and my life trimmed down to what I dearly loved and absolutely had to do, I designed a tool to help me keep information written down rather than taking up space in my head—to make mental margin for myself. Relying on this little tool to help sort out the have-tos and the want-tos

Who says
you have to be
so **BUSY** *all*
the time?

gave me a peace of mind I'd never felt before. It didn't feel like just another task to complete; instead, my Simplified Planner gave me a fresh start every day.

Now that it's caught on, I enjoy seeing customers use our tool and hearing from users who love its gold details and simple features. It makes me so proud of our team. But it's not a magic fix. The planner itself doesn't fill my heart to its brim. I know firsthand that our problem isn't our lack of an awesome planner; it's the abundance of things on our schedules. The battle for our hearts is won when we strip our schedules down to the raw essentials—the things that truly fire us up. It's won when we budget our minutes like we budget dollars: carefully and with consideration. We find happiness when we say yes to white space and no to the extra—when we choose the good over the perfect.

AN INTENTIONAL CALENDAR

At certain times in life, our calendars are slam full. We're working our fingers to the bone to keep food on the table and are stretched thin, with no relief in sight. Even in those times, I believe that being intentional with our time is key to finding joy. Every yes we say is a choice to say no to something that is a lower priority, but sometimes we don't have the luxury of making those choices. When you can't say no to the things that matter, like working those extra hours to pay the health insurance premium, perhaps you can choose some small yeses to make the burden somewhat lighter. Even the tiniest yes can make a big difference. Saying yes to letting your kids make a mess means saying yes to adventure and creativity, which might make the burden you're carrying feel lighter and glittered with fun and laughter. Saying yes to accepting help from friends means filling your well ever so slightly and allowing your village to rally for you when you need them. Perhaps the biggest no you could say in the middle of times of stress is, "No, I will not feel guilty that these necessary commitments are part of our lives right now." Extend yourself some grace.

> *Life may be messy, but the mess is worth it.*

Try this. Make a list of everything that is fighting for your time and attention: clubs, schools, sports, volunteer organizations, committees, work—everything. Make your list, check it twice, and give everything that isn't top priority a good strikethrough. Just because you're good at something or just because something is a noble cause doesn't mean it needs your attention right now. Take ten minutes, and make a few phone calls or send a few e-mails. Quit. It's okay to be a quitter when you're choosing what matters.

CHECKLIST

Make a list of your commitments. Cross out the ones that can go. Take ten minutes and quit.

_____

_____

_____

_____

_____

_____

However you do it, give yourself the gift of margin. Start with self-reflection, and then make sure your calendar reflects yourself.

Chapter 5

SURRENDERING CONTROL

Many are the plans in a person's heart,
but it is Lord's purpose that prevails.

PROVERBS 19:21

I SAT IN THE Chick-fil-A parking lot checking my e-mail after breakfast. I'd spent the morning catching up with two old friends over Chick-n-Minis. It had been a wonderful few days back home in Pensacola, Florida, visiting my family and friends to show them my newly protruding baby belly. I was nearing five months pregnant with Brady. I pressed Play on a voice mail I'd received earlier that morning.

"Mrs. Ley," said a woman whose voice I instantly recognized as my obstetrician's, "I need to speak with you right away regarding your recent test results. Please call me as soon as possible."

My stomach dropped as I hurriedly dialed her number. Sitting in my car that morning, I learned that a simple screening test had revealed concerning numbers indicating that our precious first baby could have spina bifida—a serious birth defect also known as "cleft spine." My OB referred us to a doctor who specialized in high-risk pregnancies for a particular kind of ultrasound to check our baby's spine.

I was so confused. I'd done everything right. We'd been seeing a doctor for a year while we struggled with infertility. I ate all the right things. I avoided all the wrong things. I read up on pregnancy and educated myself on everything possible. That evening, while being comforted by my parents, I frantically Googled new words that I didn't understand. Every search result seemed to make my worries a little more intense. My anxiety grew, and I decided to cut my trip short.

The following afternoon, as we waited for our names to be called in the waiting room at the specialist's office, Bryan and I tried to avoid eye contact with other worried parents-to-be. Finally, a sonographer brought us to the ultrasound room. She rolled the cold wand over my belly, revealing my sweet boy's face on the monitor. My heart melted at the sight. His tiny hands moved back and forth as the sonographer tried to get him to turn to reveal his back. Bryan and I exchanged worried glances when we realized she wasn't going to give us any information during the exam.

We studied the live sonogram, looking for any clues we

could find. After a few minutes, the tech left with the results, and the doctor walked into the room. We traded fast hellos as he quickly glanced over my chart and asked for a second sonogram. Matter-of-factly, he turned to us and said, "Your baby does not have spina bifida. But he may have achondroplasia, also known as dwarfism."

Every ounce of blood in my body rushed to my toes as I tried to process his words one by one. Stunned, I looked at Bryan, as if pleading with him to fix it. Bryan calmly asked the doctor to explain. While our sweet boy's body was in the ninety-eighth percentile, his femurs measured in the second to third percentile. The doctor ran through a battery of other possibilities, pointing out symptoms we'd need to look for, tests that needed to be run, and other findings he'd noticed. But my brain had tuned out. My heart was broken for my sweet boy and terrified of what this could mean for him. I asked the doctor what I could eat or do or what supplements I could take to help with my baby's growth. He kindly told me nothing I'd done or could do would change the outcome.

Bryan and I left that appointment a mess of worry and tears. We were confused and frightened. Over the next few months, we went to appointment after appointment and had ultrasounds almost every week. Our doctor continued to check for characteristics that could add up to an eventual diagnosis. Oddly, though, Brady didn't have many of the hallmark signs they were looking for. But with every visit, they discovered other unexplainable concerns that added to the mystery. Our doctor finally said to me, "Emily, these findings could mean that something is very wrong. Or they could all be anomalies. We won't have an answer until he is born."

EMBRACE THE STORY

I grieved a lot during those last few months of my pregnancy. I grieved for the normal pregnancy I'd prayed for for years. I grieved for the life our child might have. And I grieved for the other mamas and daddies who'd sat in similar waiting rooms and received diagnoses far more tragic. I grieved over the fact that I couldn't control the outcome of the situation. My entire life, I'd thought that if I worked hard at something, I could get it. A certain level of sacrifice and hard work would result in the desired achievement. But in this situation, nothing I did could help or change the little boy growing inside me.

A month before Brady was born, I sat in a roomful of close girlfriends and shared my fears. I cried over the way the world might treat Brady. I cried because he might look different than other kids. I cried because I worried for his health. I cried because the situation was totally out of my control and I couldn't do anything to help him. I held my belly and felt his little kicks against my palms. My friend Stefanie reached over and handed me a note. It read,

For you created my inmost being; you knit me together in my mother's womb. I praise you because I am fearfully and wonderfully made; your works are wonderful, I know that full well. My frame was not hidden from you when I was made in the secret place, when I was woven together in the depths of the earth. (Psalm 139:13–15)

God knew what He was doing that night. Those words soaked into my heart, and He gave me an indescribable peace for the next thirty days. I knew that no matter what happened, there would be no surprises for God. That comforted my weary heart, which had been stockpiling worry for months.

Late one evening in mid-February, I showered and quietly listened to Adele sing a song called "Make You Feel My Love." Salty tears of surrender flowed down my face as I gave the Lord control over the next twenty-four hours. Because of the concerns for Brady's health, I was induced on my due date. And after seventeen hours of labor, I was wheeled to the operating room to prepare for a C-section.

I like to be in charge (I'm sure this is surprising). And so many times in life, I've shaken my fists at God and told Him that if He'd just listen to me, He'd see that my plan is really, really good. But nothing about becoming a mother had gone according to my plans. I dreamed of a surprise conception; God allowed infertility. I dreamed of a glowing pregnancy; God allowed forty weeks of uncertainty. I dreamed of experiencing the miracle of birth, squeezing my husband's hand, pushing Brady into the world; God allowed a C-section.

It was almost surreal, staring at the white ceiling of the operating room, listening to my doctor prep the nurses for Brady's birth. She read a list of concerns that could, in just a few short minutes, either equal a diagnosis or all be attributed to coincidence. In that moment, I wanted to run. I told my legs to get off that table and run out the door. I didn't want to do it. I wasn't ready to know. I just wanted my mom. My legs didn't listen, as you can imagine. I'd given everything up to God, so all I could really do was believe that He was in control.

> *So many times I've shaken my fists at God and told Him that if He'd just listen to me, He'd see that my plan is really, really good.*

Bryan walked into the room wearing scrubs, as nervous as I was. He was wearing a ratty LSU hat under his scrub cap. I remember being perplexed about why he was wearing a hat in the operating room. Bryan's smarter than me. He knew he'd distract me from my fears with that silly thing. He smiled from beneath his mask and told me how beautiful our son would be and how excited he was to meet him. I pleaded with him to take me out of there. He squeezed my hand, our sign for *I love you.*

My doctor came to my side of the curtain and asked me if I was ready. A nurse strapped my arms straight out to my sides—an ironic position of surrender. I closed my eyes and, in that moment, I knew that no matter who Brady was, I already loved him with every bit of my heart. I knew that God had given him to me specifically and had prepared me be his mother. I was ready. A few short minutes later, I felt my doctor shake my hips. And then, a cry. I looked at Bryan as he peered over the curtain.

"Hi," he said quietly.

Before I could ask, my doctor came to my side of the curtain again.

"Emily," she said, close to tears herself. "He's beautiful. He's healthy. And he has really long legs."

I don't remember anything else. Other than the anesthesiologist pressing on my arm, telling me to breathe. Apparently, sobbing isn't good when you're under anesthesia. Bryan tried to explain why I was so emotional as she sedated me.

TRUST

Brady has been a perfectly healthy, very tall little boy his entire life. No one can explain the anomalies of his ultrasounds. Except me. Enormous things changed in my heart during the nine months I was pregnant. I was broken down and built together again into a new woman. I lost control in a way I'd never experienced before. It wasn't in the resolution of it all when I felt God the most; it was in the quiet moments in the middle of the night, when fear overtook me. He met me there. For some reason, He needed to push me to 7:21 P.M. that evening when Brady was born. He changed me. And from that minute, I've never been the same.

Our need to be in control, to orchestrate the perfect scenario for every journey of our lives, breeds anxiety in our hearts. We try to do the right things, eat the right things, say the right things to get the results we hope for. Our inability to trust that it will be okay, even if all the pieces of the puzzle don't fit just right, can lead to comparison, worry, and unhappiness. Sometimes there is greater gladness in the mess than if everything had gone "according to plan." In my mess, I found quiet, connected moments with my husband. I learned what it means to have unwavering faith. I learned that family is everything, as my mom researched with me and my dad told jokes to lighten the mood. But more than anything, I learned what it means to let go. Those few minutes on the operating table taught me that no amount of empty hustle, no amount of Internet searches, no amount of perfection could bring me ultimate joy. The joy is in the journey, even the hard ones.

With each piece of the puzzle we release, we find true freedom and true joy. When we're able to let the pieces fall where they will, we free our hands for better purposes.

MY THOUGHTS

Which imperfect puzzle are you trying to put together right now? Where do you need to let go? What worries are you stockpiling?

TIPS FOR LETTING GO

Identify those areas of your life where you're holding tightly to the reins.

_____

_____

_____

Think through the worst-case scenario if you loosen your grip and give in to the mess or the unknown a bit. What does it look like?

_____

_____

_____

Finally, give yourself some grace. You're doing a good job! Perfect isn't always best.

GRACE WITH YOURSELF

Your body is a vessel of love, and your heart is a well. Neglect yourself, and your heart will run dry. Care for yourself, as you would a loved one, and your heart will brim with the good stuff of life: patience, love, kindness, and empathy.

Perfection is overrated. There is joy in the mess, the circus, and the seventh load of laundry if you allow yourself to be still enough to see it.

Grace is an outstretched hand, ready to deliver you from the hamster wheel of trying to do it all.

Part 2

GRACE WITH YOUR PEOPLE

I AM SO GRATEFUL God doesn't make me do this crazy life alone. Even though our relationships aren't perfect, how awesome is it that He gives us spouses, parents, siblings, friends, and children? Believe it or not, your presence on this earth has an incalculable influence on those lives. As perfectly imperfect human beings, we're constantly impacting, affecting, and influencing other people. What a great responsibility. When we keep that in mind, simple conversations and passing interactions begin to carry weight. The morning rush to get everyone's shoes on becomes just as important as dinnertime conversation. The quick midday phone call from your spouse becomes just as important as pillow talk after a long day.

The way you thank the grocery bagger at the supermarket becomes as important as the way you thank an executive after a meeting at work. God's grace shines through our ability to love others with sincere patience, gratitude, and acceptance. He's not the only one dishing out grace. We have the ability (and responsibility) to deliver it as well.

So why aren't we loving *all* our people—spouses, children, family, friends, and even strangers—like there's no tomorrow? When we feel loved and included, we are accepting of others—good for good. When we are thirsty for approval, we don't use kind or affirming words with others—bad for bad. When we're overwhelmed, we misplace our anxiety and put blame on the ones we love. Even worse. It's a round-robin chicken-and-egg situation.

What if we unabashedly poured love on our loved ones and our communities, even when we don't feel like it? I don't know about you, but when I extend sincere courtesy and perform random acts of kindness, my heart suddenly feels fuller. And before I know it, I've filled that well up with more of the good stuff—more for me to pour out. What a beautiful circle *that* is.

The first step to deepening our relationships and fostering beautiful experiences with the people we love is simple: *love them*. Love them with big, unapologetic, awkward, whole-hearted love. Love others like the One who loves you. Start the good cycle of filling up your well by intentionally filling up someone else's. Say the things you're tempted to keep inside. Give the hugs. Be an includer. Let everyone have a seat at the table. In this section, we'll talk about what it means to have grace with our spouses, kids, friends, and communities while having grace with ourselves. We'll explore ways to open our hearts to receive God's enormous grace so that we can then pour that love and grace on others. That freedom will give us space for what matters more than anything on this earth: love and grace for our people.

God's grace shines through our ability to love others with sincere patience, gratitude, and acceptance.

Chapter 6

INVEST IN YOUR PERSON

Love never fails.

I CORINTHIANS 13:8

SPOUSES PLAY AN INCREDIBLE role in our lives as our part-ner, helper, encourager, and friend. And while the principles of this chapter apply deeply to marriages, they also apply beau-tifully to other important relationships, even for unmarried women and single mothers. Each big and small relationship in our lives, no matter its nature, affects our minds, our time, and our hearts. Whatever stage of life you find yourself in right now, know this simple and unchanging truth: *love never fails.*

When I was twenty-four, a boy I'd cared about for a long time put a ring on my finger. In the middle of a Panera. I was covered in ink, halfway through a grad-school project, when he hit his knee and asked me the big question. A few months later, I stood in a three-way mirror on top of a wooden box, wearing a gorgeous lace wedding gown. It was a top contender for "the one." I'd done all the right things in the right order: graduate from high school, go to college, go to grad school, get a great job, get engaged. With all the perfect pieces of my perfect puzzle in place, I expected this moment to feel equally perfect. It was simple math: perfect plan equals perfect outcome. But it wasn't adding up. My high school sweetheart and I called off our wedding that weekend.

For thirteen whole days, I felt like my world was over. I was the "un-engaged" girl. After dating for ten years, I suddenly felt divorced. And for many reasons, I didn't know who I was anymore. But only for thirteen days. One evening, a good friend called and told me someone from out of town wanted to see me at the restaurant they were at together. I told her I didn't care and I was perfectly fine growing old alone with twelve cats.

"It's Bryan Ley," she said.

"Oh," I said. I quickly got dressed and put on my makeup. That was the only name that could have convinced me.

God's funny like that. When He strips us of all the things that make us feel safe and secure, He gives us a story far better than we could have written for ourselves. Bryan and I had worked at the same restaurant seven years prior. I'd always thought he had a cute smile. And he was funny. Really funny. One evening, during a shift together, Bryan brought me a *Sesame Street* car with Ernie driving. A little boy had left it

*When God strips
us of all the things
that make us feel*

SAFE *and*

SECURE,

*He gives us a story far
better than we could have
written for ourselves.*

on one of his tables. He told me it was a gift for me, from him. I giggled and probably rolled my eyes and told him he was ridiculous. But I stuck it in my pocket. I thought he was a really, really great guy—a perfect catch even—at sixteen.

Eight months after we made contact again, the man who made me laugh harder than anyone I'd ever known, who challenged me to be braver and better, who showed me for the first time what big, endless, selfless love looks like, asked me to be his wife. Without hesitation, I said yes. Ordinarily, at a momentous occasion like this, I'd think to call my mom or post to Facebook or snap a great picture to document the occasion. But in that moment, all I wanted to do was savor the experience. For an hour, Bryan and I talked about our future, about my impending move, and about our wedding—before we told anyone we were engaged. He told me the story of how he'd had the ring custom-made for me and shipped to his office. He'd been so nervous it would be lost in transit. Those moments were some of the most precious of my life because we chose to savor them.

CHOOSE WHAT'S IMPORTANT

In marriage, we're continually choosing each other, even when life is busy, even when we drive each other nuts. In a home with two parents, I strongly believe that the marriage steers the family. My children will be immeasurably formed by my relationship with

Bryan, so we make it a priority. They hear the way I speak to him and the way he speaks to me. They see the way I do or do not stop to give him a hug when he gets home from work. Their first experiences with grace are going to be the way they observe it in their parents when they disagree. They observe how we handle momentous occasions and everyday arguments.

That said, Bryan and I are polar opposites. I love healthy food and a neat house. Bryan loves pizza and doesn't even notice that the laundry's piled up. I'm a planner. Bryan is spontaneous. I love broccoli. Bryan hates broccoli. But God made our lives more fun when He put us together. Bryan challenges me and pushes me. Because of him, I've had experiences I never would have otherwise—including being an entrepreneur. And because of me, Bryan's discovered the benefits of structure and tradition. We may be different in many areas, but we chose each other because our hearts are in line. We choose God together. We choose to put our family first. We choose funny movies and blueberry bagels and chips and queso. (No seriously, we are queso connoisseurs.) But above all that, we choose each other day after crazy day.

KEEPING LOVE ALIVE

If we love each other so much, why is it so easy for us to snap at each other? I'm a nonconfrontational person. I cringe at the thought of disagreeing with someone outside my four walls. But if Bryan leaves his socks on the floor, I am quick to let him know. Bryan knows me better than just about anyone. He's my person. We handle every major life event together. We see each other at our best and at our worst. And after a while, we can take each other for granted and hold each other to higher standards than we hold ourselves. So how do we give more grace to our person?

1. **Start with yourself.** Happiness breeds happiness. If you've embraced your own imperfections, you'll be able to embrace your spouse's imperfections. No one's perfect.

2. **Get specific.** If you're upset about something, name it. Just because you're angry that the dishwasher's not been emptied for three days doesn't mean you're angry about your spouse's character. You're angry about his choices in the last three days, which could have any number of reasons behind them. Don't mix that up with his worth as a person. These kinds of arguments can be detrimental.

3. **Be a lover.** Okay, now before you start thinking rose petals and candlelight, consider this: a *lover* is defined as "someone who loves." And *Merriam-Webster* defines *love* as "a feeling of warm personal attachment or deep affection." I don't know about

you, but I don't always demonstrate that in the way I act. I love Bryan, but so many times I'm so busy with work and the kids and wiping the countertops for the eighteenth time that I forget to be a lover.

4. **Save nuggets of goodness.** Sometimes life is really good, and sometimes life is really hard. Take photos. Save mementos from special dates, even when you're no longer technically dating. (And by the way, keep dating! Even after you're married.) Keep a box of treasures under your bed to rifle through when life is mundane or hard. Physical reminders of happy times bring back joyful feelings in any relationship.

Having grace with your person is hard sometimes, whether your person is your spouse, a family member, or a best friend. Intentionally pouring into that person and allowing a standard of grace in your relationship goes a long way.

GIVE LOVE

On the first fall day of 2008, Bryan and I got married in a little white church in downtown Pensacola. The weather was beautiful: perfectly clear and seventy degrees. Before the ceremony, I nestled a handwritten note and a small gift into a little box and handed it to my maid of honor to take to Bryan.

We couldn't see each other before the wedding, of course. She went across the street to the church where Bryan and his groomsmen were putting on their boutonnieres. Inside that box was a promise to choose him every day of our lives and "to make memories that will be talked about on rocking chairs one day, memories as special as this one." Tucked beneath the note was the *Sesame Street* car he'd given me when I was sixteen. He didn't know I'd saved it.

That memory is a nugget of goodness that I've packed away deep in my heart. Some poor child may have been traumatized losing that toy, but it sure became special to us! I still remember the depth of love I felt for that man as we stood at the alter—intense and all-encompassing and full of life. But as the years went by, we had kids and got busy with our jobs, and suddenly it wasn't as easy to be as infatuated with each other as we once were. That doesn't mean we love each other any less. It just means our little romance got thrown into real life.

Through some of the happiest and hardest moments of our lives, our love has grown thick and strong and weathered. It's old and beautiful, and it serves as a blanket when life gets cold. We love each other to death, but we also drive each other bananas sometimes (sound familiar?). Along the way, we've learned some practical things that work for us and make us a better team and that allow love to grow instead of waste away.

Schedule At-Home Date Nights

With three kids and busy jobs, nights out on the town are few and far between. Plus, we're both exhausted by seven o'clock. We have a tendency to go our separate ways when we're tired, but we started making intentional at-home date nights with to-go tacos and a few episodes of *Shark Tank*. Something as simple as shoulder-to-shoulder time on the couch is like money in the bank for us. Just knowing that we're still "us," regardless of everything we are to everyone else, makes us better.

Establish Routines and Traditions

Establishing routines and traditions is critically important for us (we'll talk more about it later in the book). Do you ever feel like you're doing *everything* and your spouse is doing *nothing*? That's probably not the case, but it sure can feel like that sometimes—for both of us. And those unsaid feelings breed resentment. I borrowed a trick from my mom once and wrote all the household responsibilities out on sticky notes. I laid them out, and we each chose a few until they were all gone. And to this day, we still take care of the chores we chose back then. Now we've gotten in a groove where he always takes the trash out and I always empty the dishwasher. We also decided to outsource a few things like mowing the lawn. Yes, that costs money, but we consider it an investment in our family because it frees up time for us to do something fun together on the weekends.

Give Each Other Space

This might sound counterintuitive, but it is so important. We need time away from each other sometimes to invest in ourselves. Bryan needs time away from me and my chatterbox self to unwind and play golf or watch *SportsCenter.* I need an hour every now and then to watch *Gilmore Girls* or search for amazing shoes at the mall. It's taken time to get to a place where we can recognize when the other needs a break from our life. Typically, after the kiddos go to bed, we go our separate ways for a while and come back together to talk or watch TV before we go to bed. It's become a routine and helps us unwind. Create a healthy balance, and reserve space for your mind to grow and rest on its own.

Pick Your Battles

Just like socks on the floor don't equal major character flaws, dishes in the sink shouldn't always equal an argument. Pick your battles. We were rookies at this during our first year of marriage, and we drove each other nuts nitpicking at every little thing. It didn't take us long to realize that every transgression didn't need to be hashed out. It's all about showing grace and allowing each other to be human.

We've learned this through trial, error, and good advice from those who have been married longer than us. This creates an environment where we can be healthy as individuals and as a couple.

BE A MEMORY MAKER

One of the most important things someone once told me about marriage is this: you are responsible for the way you'll look back on your life when you're eighty years old. You're in control of the way you'll feel that day in your rocking chair on your front porch. And you are also responsible for the way your spouse will feel. That's a big deal.

Aside from our children, one of the greatest gifts Bryan has ever given me is supporting my dream to design the Simplified Planner. While Bryan holds a full-time job in commercial insurance, he still manages the finances for our company during his off time. Together, we ran our brand design company debt-free. But in 2013, I wanted to take all the money we had in the business bank account and invest it in a product and mission I cared deeply about: creating a simple planner to help overwhelmed women make more time for what really matters in life. Here's what Bryan had to go on when we made that decision together:

- Emily is currently a brand designer and, although she's sold one-off personalized planners in the past, she wants to leave a fantastic graphic design income to create a product that isn't guaranteed to turn a profit en masse and try to sell it full time.
- Emily has no idea how to manufacture planners in bulk.
- Emily believes in this wholeheartedly.

He agreed to support my decision as I took all six thousand dollars in our business bank account to produce the first Simplified Planners.

And he helped me walk each of those first hardcover Simplified Planners to the curb for the recycling company to pick up. Because of my inexperience in production, they were all printed incorrectly. But he encouraged me, and I tried again. And I got it right that time. And we built a business out of it. When I'm eighty years old and look back on my life, I will be grateful for the way I was able to live out my dream because of Bryan's unwavering support, even when I fell on my face.

WAYS TO SERVE YOUR PERSON WITH GRACE

1. Plan regular time together. Make it a tradition: Friday at-home date night or Monday morning coffee or lunch together once a month at your favorite spot.
2. Ask your person how you can support him or her. What does he or she want to look back on in life and remember? What does he or she hope the highlights are?
3. Talk through tactical things you can do now to make those highlights reality.

Chapter 7

SAVOR THE CIRCUS

The days are long, but the years are short.

GRETCHEN RUBIN

I WAS ABOUT THREE chapters into writing this book one afternoon when I took a break to zip into the closet and grab another load of laundry before the babies woke up from their nap. I'd heard the washer buzzer while I was typing away and knew I could spare exactly forty-three seconds to get that next batch of towels in. Running through the bathroom, I kicked over a rogue glass of lemonade Brady must have left on the floor. Lemonade soaked the bath mat and the clothes he'd piled on the floor from his bath the night before. I considered cuss words but chose tears instead. I was at max capacity for the day. I kneeled down and put my head on the side of the bathtub, looking down at my navy blue leggings with smashed peas smeared down the side of them. *How did I get here? What gives?*

I sat on the floor for a little while, my eyes full of frustrated tears. I just wanted ten minutes to myself, and now after handling the lemonade issue I didn't even have time to put towels in and get back to writing. I could hear the babies stirring upstairs. How was I going to accomplish all I needed to do over the next few days? Nothing seemed to add up or shake out right. I could feel myself starting to spiral. I could say only one thing to myself to put it all in perspective: "This is just the season of life you're in, Emily," I told myself. "It'll be over before you know it."

Our time with little ones is so fleeting. It's both the fastest and slowest time of our lives. And for many of us, beginning motherhood coincides with a lot of other important life milestones. Our careers may be taking off. Our parents are getting older. We have big responsibilities and so many things beeping and buzzing to notify us that we're needed. Our minds are consumed with bills, to-do lists, behavior issues, comparisons, and attempts at doing everything just right. And all the while, our little ones are growing another quarter of an inch. Their chubby thighs are slimming. Their wobbly walks are steadying. If we don't purposefully and intentionally slow down, free our hands, walk away, and say no, this precious, messy season of life will pass us by.

If we don't intentionally **SLOW** *down, this precious, messy season* *will* **PASS** *us by.*

GIVE IN TO THE MESS

I gave up on the towels that day. I gave in to the circus that is life with three kids under five, and I let the craziness win. Sometimes that's the best way I can give myself grace. I put everything down and chose the only thing that truly matters: my family.

My friend Rachel Shingleton once said, "We're all juggling a lot of balls in the air. And when things get hectic, sometimes something has to give. You can drop any of those balls. But you can't drop family." Never have I heard truer words.

My solution when life gets too crazy is to throw in the lemonade-soaked towel. E-mail can wait another day. Laundry, dishes, groceries, and errands can wait another day. Picnics outside, pushing little ones on the swing, reading a sixth bedtime story . . . ? Those things can't wait. And those little faces? They're changing, and I don't want to miss out. There's something wild and freeing about just letting all the balls drop and grabbing on to the one thing that matters.

When we multitask, we think we're accomplishing two things at once. But honestly, can we ever successfully multitask? I don't believe multitasking exists. We're either doing one thing or another, constantly shifting our focus back and forth. In reality, trying to do it all always ends up in robbing one activity or task of your attention to give to the other. Have you ever tried to work on a project with unsupervised kids in the room? You know exactly what I'm talking about.

We're all after the elusive state of *balance* in our lives, whatever that is. But I have news for all of us—no one has ever really achieved it! Sure, we have moments of peace, of thinking, *I've got this!* We might feel at those moments like we know the secrets of the universe. But how long does that last really? I believe we're all better off settling into the circus— learning how to be comfortable in the sideshow. It's a blessed relief.

How many of you would have heart palpitations if I sat you in front of a sink of dirty dishes for half an hour and told you that you couldn't do a thing about it? I would! It's just in our nature to keep going and going. We're always pushing forward, always getting better, always striving to button up one more part of our lives. But when we set our eyes on reaching places where we have it all together, we might miss the delights of the little messes right in front of our eyes.

THE BEST DECORATOR

When we moved into our new home, I tried a million ways to store all the Fisher-Price paraphernalia that had taken over my old living room. This was my chance to have a beautiful living room like the ones in *House Beautiful* magazine! I stuffed the baby bouncers in the closet and the toys in a chic wooden box, and I hid the blocks in the bedrooms. Finally! A gorgeous, uncluttered living room! Now try to picture three kids who are bored sitting in a *House Beautiful* living room. The gorgeousness didn't last long. As we settled in, the baby bouncers found new homes next to the couch, and toys continually decorated my beautiful rug. And . . . I started to find the beauty in it. Could primary colors be a workable living-room palette?

I choose the messy floor because it means happy babies are discovering new motor skills and new affections on it. I choose Brady's books covering the coffee table because it's the place where he's learning to read. Choosing grace over perfection is about giving yourself permission to let go and settle in. Who wants to live in a constant state of frenzy from trying to have it all together all the time? Why scurry behind our kids, picking up their toys, rather than sitting in front of them, watching their little fingers discover new ways to move?

> *We're all better off settling into the circus—learning how to be comfortable in the sideshow.*

When we multitask our way through the sweetest parts of life, we miss the tiniest joys hidden in the moments between the grand accomplishments. It can feel like we're all bustling around as busy as bees, waiting for someone to tell us it's okay to sit down. So here it is: Free your hands. Lock the phone in a drawer. Everything else can wait.

Make a list of five messes or tasks that you are continually struggling to tackle. Beside each mess, list a sweeter activity that will give you time with those you love. Give yourself permission to make that choice at least once this week.

1. _____   _____

2. _____   _____

3. _____   _____

4. _____   _____

5. _____   _____

The e-mails will wait, but your little ones will soon forget the stories they wanted to tell you about their day. The breakfast dishes will wait, but your babies will need you to tie their shoes only a few months longer. The laundry can be folded later, but those tiny hearts need your attention *right now* if they are to heal from harsh words from a friend. I feel a deep sense of urgency about this, along with the desire to sit perfectly still and not miss a thing with my kids. All too soon, they won't want me to tuck them in at night. They won't want another story (after we've read three). And they won't need Mama to kiss their knees when they fall down. Now is the time to empty my hands so I can reach out to them.

NOTICE THE SWEETNESS

When Brady was three, we found out we were expecting twins. Though we'd been undergoing fertility treatments, the news still came as a shock. But the surprise wasn't as intense as the unbelievable morning sickness that followed. Let me rephrase: all-day-and-all-night sickness. There were days when I couldn't even pick my head up off the pillow long enough to get Brady dressed for school. It was miserable, to say the least.

Three months into my pregnancy, we headed to the beach for a much-needed weeklong vacation we'd planned before we knew the twins were coming. We stayed at our favorite beachfront hotel in a beautiful room with gorgeous views of the pristine gulf. The day we arrived, I had plans for snow cones at the pool, treasure hunts on the shore, and our favorite grilled-cheese sandwiches for lunch at the waterside restaurant.

Instead I spent the entire week sick in bed. I felt so much guilt that I wasn't able to join in on all the fun things we'd planned with Brady that I cried every day. But every after-noon at three, sun-kissed, salty, sweet little Brady traded his swimsuit for a much-too-large T-shirt from our favorite Pensacola Beach restaurant and climbed into bed with me for an afternoon nap. I still remember the way the bed bounced as he bounded up to me from the bottom. He would wiggle into the cool cotton covers and share the day's adventures with me. And somewhere between stories of seashells, crabs, and too many strawberry snow cones, his little eyelids would droop and he'd fall fast asleep.

Those afternoon naps with Brady are some of my sweetest memories of my pregnancy with our twins. For a couple hours, my guilt, worry, and ruined plans fell away. Brady and I snuggled up together, the sound of the waves crashing outside our open patio door. Nothing else really mattered. Late in the trip, snuggled up with my buddy, I realized I hadn't let him down. In fact, I was exactly who he needed me to be on that trip: his snuggle buddy at nap time. I may not have been the one to go down the waterslide with him, but I was the one he got to share all his wild stories with. In those moments when we give ourselves the grace to let everything else fall away, we find our most sincere happiness.

> *In those moments when we give ourselves the grace to let everything else fall away, we find our most sincere happiness.*

GO, GO, GO, AIRPLANE

When Brady was two, we enrolled him in swimming lessons. We live in Florida and we have a pool in our backyard, so it seemed necessary. Though Brady is a pretty easygoing kid, he didn't love those swimming lessons. The teacher challenged him and made him try things he was afraid of (like getting his face wet). And every day I sat on the side of the pool and cheered him on. Though it pained me to see him so sad and afraid, I knew it was something he had to go through.

"You can do it, B!" I'd say from the steps every time he got ready for a new challenge. He'd smile through tears and give it his best shot. And little by little, Brady learned how to swim.

A few weeks after swimming lessons were over, we decided to ditch our Saturday to-do list and go to an air show so that Brady (who loves airplanes) could see how they fly. It had just begun to rain, and the air show crew scurried around to make sure everything was safe for the airplanes and the pilots. Brady, high up on his daddy's shoulders, picked up on the commotion and got a little worried for the first airplane. He'd been able to see and touch that particular airplane up close before it was transported to the field. As the rain began to fall a little harder and the airplane engine began to roar its way down the runway, I looked over at Brady's worried face.

Just as the airplane picked up enough speed to lift its nose off the ground, Brady balled his little fists up and yelled, "Go, go, go, airplane! You can *do it*!" Bryan and I turned to each other, and all my happy tears escaped my eyes. Though I thought I was just cheering Brady on at swimming lessons a few weeks earlier, I'd really taught him how to believe in himself, how to muster strength to do something hard, and how to encourage others. Who knew?

I tucked that little nugget of goodness away—it's one of those memories I'll treasure forever. And I learned a few things that afternoon:

- Our kids are learning even when we don't think they are.
- Our kids are going to mimic our attitudes, for better or worse.
- Giving our kids a spirit of confidence is one of the most special gifts we can give them.

Although parenting is full of sweet, special moments, it's also full of difficult, challenging ones. For example, Brady recently learned how to roll his eyes. I have to hold back laughter as I teach him that it's not an appropriate response when Mommy asks him to do something. Seriously, imagine that little boy, hand on hip, a giant eye-roll, complete with sound effects. Clearly it's a learned behavior. And sometimes, when I've had *just* enough of the craziness and that eye-roll threatens to push me over the edge of impatience and lost tempers, I remember how much that little sponge of mine picks up. So instead, I model the *right* behaviors, to show him what should happen when life doesn't go our way.

And I'll be honest, there are a *lot* of days when life doesn't go my way. By five o'clock every evening, after a full workday, I'm on my own with three kids under the age of five until Bryan gets home. Inevitably, someone's wearing half the clothes they should be, someone's hungry and begging for macaroni and cheese / PBJ / an ice-cream sundae, someone's screaming, and someone's desperate for Daddy to get home. I keep my mom on speed dial and a stash of chocolate hidden way in the back of the freezer for these very moments. I find myself praying for more patience—even when I feel like I've scraped up every ounce I have.

And although this chapter is all about kiddos, so much can be said for having grace with other loved ones we hold near and dear—parents, siblings, best friends, and close co-workers. I have to go back to the actual definition of *grace* with each of these relationships: "the unmerited favor of God toward humanity." Each of these special people in our lives, whether children or family members or peers, is flawed. They are imperfect, fallible humans. Just like us! And as God pours His unwavering, undeserved grace on us, it's our job to have grace with one another. I really believe that delivering grace says more about the deliverer than the recipient. The grace giver is patient, forgiving, and overflowing with love. Her well is deep and wide and full of the good stuff necessary for acting in grace.

Who could you have more grace with in your life? How can you love him or her, even when it's difficult? List three people close to you and ways you can love them unconditionally.

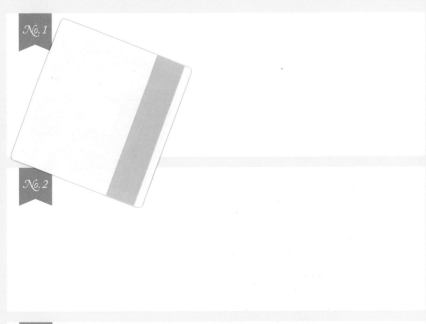

No. 1

No. 2

No. 3

Chapter 8

YOUR COMMUNITY

Sometimes the best way to make
friends is second-grade style.

IT'S EASY TO FEEL alone when you're in the thick of it—to feel like no one else in the world understands the battles you fight or the life you live. But this idea—that no one else can relate—can keep us from living in community and from feeling understood and connected. We're all dealing with so many hang-ups when it comes to community. We're worried we won't be accepted if we try to connect. Or we're afraid of how hard we'll have to try to make friends. Sometimes it feels easier to be alone and to stick to what we know.

I often find myself fighting the idea that every woman already has enough friends. Plus I make up all sorts of inferiority fantasies like, *Oh, she surely has a homemade dinner on the table at six every night, all while earning accolades at work with perfectly curled hair and six-inch heels. I don't even remember how to walk in heels after three kids. What could she want with an imperfect girl who forgets her friends' birthdays sometimes and might forget diapers if invited to a playdate?* We all buy in to the lie that other women, especially the ones we admire, have it all together. And that's keeping us from feeling the love and warmth of community—the close community God deeply desires for us.

When I moved to Tampa after Bryan and I got married, I knew absolutely no one and found myself feeling pretty lonely in the friend department. It took three years of awkward conversations and transient friendships for me to realize what was keeping me from genuine community. It wasn't my not-so-perfect house or the fact that I wore the wrong clothes. It was that although I was trying to measure up and to be worthy of good friends, I was trying to connect on all the wrong levels, be it gossip or complaining or talking about all of my material wants. It wasn't until I allowed myself to be totally imperfect in front of strangers that I found real, genuine friendships.

The women who became my dearest friends in my new town saw me cry in department stores over toddler tantrums or when I was unable to keep up my "with-it" image. They saw me sob over breastfeeding woes and told me how great I looked immediately post-birth (bless them) because they knew I needed to hear it. They knew my flaws, and they cheered me on despite them—perhaps because they recognized themselves in those flaws. We connected on levels that were vulnerable, real, and imperfect. I really believe many of my friendships blossomed because I allowed myself to be *me*. That type of sincerity levels the playing field and puts us all right where we should be: in the same boat. It's so easy to make friends when we're all seeing each other eye to eye.

Do you ever feel like that freshman in knee-highs, glancing from her lunch tray to a room of full tables, trying to find a seat while minimizing her awkwardness? We all want a seat at the table, but we're waiting for someone to stand up, wave us over, and invite us in. In the age of everything fast-paced and high-speed, it's still up to us to create community the old-fashioned way. It takes awkward encounters, continually showing up, and putting ourselves out there. And as much as we like to think we can go it alone, *we need friends*. We might think we're too busy to make an effort, but God wants friendship for us. He wants us to feel understood and heard. He wants us to have the joy that comes with real face time.

In late 2012, I found real friendship in its truest form. Simplified Planner sales were growing, but we couldn't afford to hire a fulfillment house quite yet (someone to pack and ship all our boxes). Instead, some of my friends heard about how overwhelmed we were trying to ship planners out of my living room and decided to come over and help. They knew I could pay them only a little (plus cheese-and-cracker lunches around my kitchen island). We liked to call it *charcuterie*, but it's really just cheese and crackers. Those sweet friends showed up for me, even when insisted I could do it myself. They knew I was working well into the evenings, sometimes later, and that I really needed a break. Together we shipped truckloads of planners in mere days. Little bitty Brady even slapped our signature colorful YAY! stickers onto each box before it departed for the post office. What memories those days are for me! Our friendships blossomed so much because these people showed up for me, no questions asked. Friendship and community are so much about just that—showing up.

> *Two are better than one, because they have a good reward for their toil. For if they fall, one will lift up his fellow. But woe to him who is alone when he falls and has not another to lift him up! Again, if two lie together, they keep warm, but how can one keep warm alone? And though a man might prevail against one who is alone, two will withstand him—a threefold cord is not quickly broken.*
>
> —ECCLESIASTES 4:9-12 ESV

As much as we like to think

we can go it alone,

we need **FRIENDS**.

CREATING COMMUNITY

I realized through that experience that God wanted me to learn how to make genuine friends—second-grade style. That involved me saying hi to complete strangers and thinking up reasons for us to get together (and get to know each other). I couldn't just sit around and wait for a new friend to find me; I had to put myself out there and seek community. I needed to invite them to the table! I had to show up for people unexpectedly. I looked for any way to be a friend and love on people: sending cards to a friend battling Lyme disease, taking dinner to a new mama, having dinner with a recently divorced friend even though I knew I didn't have the time. I carved out space in my life for friendship because it truly is important, and my life has been forever blessed because of the women I've connected with.

And little by little, my village began to form. Yes, it takes a village to raise a child, but it also takes a village to do life well. This little village of mine encourages me, challenges me, tells me to pick myself up when I need to, and shows up when I need them. We do that for each other. That's what villages do. They care deeply for one another.

Earlier this year, we moved into a new house. Our new neighbors kindly invited us over for dinner just a few short days after we got settled. Bryan and I were really looking forward to making new friends. We got all the kids dressed in their cutest outfits, picked up a veggie tray from the grocery store, and walked over. I was a little embarrassed by my pre-packaged veggie tray (not my usual "let-me-bring-something" appetizer) and nervous about taking three kids under five to someone's home, because that's just plain scary and unpredictable. So I packed the best diaper bag ever: four bottles, their favorite toys, blankets, and at least sixteen pacifiers. Everything we'd need to avert disaster.

As it turned out, Brady made friends with their children really quickly and ran off to play. Bryan held Caroline, and I held Tyler. We chatted and laughed and talked about the home-building process. I thought to myself, *I've got this! This mother-of-three thing is* mine. *Take that!*

And then it happened.

Tyler started to *scream*. It didn't even begin as a little cry. No way, sister. It was a downright get-me-out-of-here, how-dare-you-take-me-out-in-public siren of a cry. I batted my eyelashes a few times, bounced him on my hip, and laughed nervously (because surely he was going to calm down and prove to everyone my awesome mothering skills).

He didn't stop. My sweet middle child, three minutes older than his sister, never cries. Never ever. He is the easiest baby this side of the Mississippi. But that night he had other plans.

I started sweating and exchanging panicked looks with Bryan. Bryan nonchalantly buckled Caroline into the stroller while I used my super-calm-under-pressure voice to call Brady downstairs.

"Uhh, we'd better run. Thanks so much for having us . . ."

In my head I was screaming, *Abort! Run! They'll never invite you back!*

And run we did. All the way to our house. Funny thing is, Tyler calmed down once we put him down to sleep. And our neighbors didn't hate us. In fact, they've become close friends. We still laugh about our first get-together. In that moment though, I was certain they had never been on the receiving end of a public baby tantrum. Those things only happen to me. Right? But let me assure you: it's common to mama-kind. In the common struggles, we get closer to those around us as we open ourselves up to the empathy, laughs, and understanding that come with the occasional meltdown.

Since that day, I've realized I have to manage my expectations and be realistic about how much I can participate in during this season of my life. We don't go out to eat much as a family (because that's just plain crazy). We can't stay late when we take the whole family somewhere. That's just life right now. And that's okay. This is a season that will be gone all too soon. When I have this type of perspective, it helps me approach life—and others—a little more graciously when things don't go as planned.

Settling in to this season of my life and finding the humor in all its craziness has really helped me embrace confidence in who I am right now. And honestly, even though I still make a run for it when the kids scream in the grocery store, being able to laugh off the chaos is a really beautiful thing. Are you hiding under a rock because of your situation? Perhaps you're recently divorced or you're shy or you've gone through a life event that makes you feel alienated from others. Building community and surrounding yourself with good people is about more than just having a social life. It's about putting yourself in the right situations to meet people who make your life better—maybe they're just like you or maybe they're different. That's the beautiful thing about villages—they're diverse and full of people with many stories and strengths.

YOUR WEAKNESS CAN BE SOMEONE ELSE'S STRENGTH

As we've discussed, if you get me in a kitchen, I'm guaranteed to mess something up. I've tried really, really hard to become a good cook, but I don't have it in me. Plus, I just don't like cooking. And *that's okay.* It took me a long time to be able to say that without being flooded with guilt. I used to beat myself up about being a bad cook. While my mom, dad, and brother can easily whip up something incredible with a dash of this and a pinch of that, I'm the one sweating it out, measuring every grain of salt on the teaspoon to make sure it's not too much or too little. For whatever reason, that cooking gene passed me by.

This is often inconvenient when you love to entertain. So instead of offering amazing home-cooked dishes, I decided to accept my weakness and focus on my strength: setting a pretty table. I love design and color and playing with textures and finishes. I also love doing it on the cheap, so that adds an extra element of fun.

Here are a few choice tips from a bad cook who loves having people over: fake them all out by making a mean charcuterie board. They'll never know the difference. They'll just know that you know how to find the most delicious cheeses and olives. Also, always set out cute napkins. Paper napkins from the clearance section at Target are great. I have a stockpile in my pantry that drives my husband nuts. But they sure make any get-together feel well thought out! Also, veggie trays from the grocery store go great with a little primping on a beautiful tray. Add some nice glasses for drinks and some grapes in a bowl, and you're set. Boom. Now you have no excuse for not having people over and building or strengthening that village of yours.

HOW TO MAKE A GREAT CHARCUTERIE BOARD

1. Use a wooden cutting board or large plate.
2. Position three or four cheeses and small knives at angles. Slice off a few pieces.
3. In small dishes, place olives, nuts, and/or cured meats.

4. Lay out your cutest paper napkins and plates.
5. Done. Everyone will be so impressed!

In true community and in real, genuine friendships, no one cares if your cooking is bad or if you serve a bunch of ready-made stuff. In fact, no one cares if you order Domino's. What matters is togetherness—the idea that you're not alone, that we're all sharing meals and stories and leaving a gathering feeling just a little more joyful and connected than when we arrived. That's what true community is about.

Why beat yourself up for what you're *not* doing? Why compare yourself to others who clearly have different strengths? Why let that keep you from connecting? I'm so amazed at Brady's preschool class's room mother. She's always e-mailing, organizing, and spending time in his classroom. For a while, I felt sad that I wasn't doing more and even guilty that I hadn't signed up for her role. I considered packing my schedule and stepping up to the plate until I realized what that would do to everything else in my life (margin, please!). No, that mom was *made* to shine as a room mother extraordinaire. She's part of my community, and that's a gift—not an invitation to feel bad about myself or compare. Thank God she's there to take on that role so well!

I wish I had time to volunteer with certain organizations or speak at certain conferences. I wanted to be room mother for Brady's class this year, but the reality is that I just couldn't

It takes a **VILLAGE** to do life well.

swing it. I took on the role of team mom for Brady's soccer team instead. (Go, Sharks!) Organizing who's bringing the post-game oranges is a lot more doable for me than other commitments. And that's totally okay. It's what I'm able to do during this season of my life. Likewise, other people are at the perfect season to take up the torch in their particular areas.

You don't have to be the best at everything. Allow your weaknesses to be someone else's strengths. That's what community is for. There is nothing wrong with stepping aside for sanity's sake. Instead of stretching yourself too thin, create margin and manage your expectations about what you can handle right now. Once you stop beating yourself up for what you're not doing, you're able to be more gracious with the people you love. And you give someone else the chance to shine in the role you couldn't take on.

You don't have to completely miss out though. Serving the community can mean different things to different people at different times. Do you wish you had time to feed the homeless at your local shelter? Buy dinner for a family in need instead. Do you wish you could volunteer in your child's classroom? Do a special craft with your little one at home one evening, or ask the teacher what supplies you can send in. Do you wish you could serve more in your church? Find a quiet moment, and pray for your church leaders. Do you wish you could serve on a nonprofit board or be more involved in their mission? Skip your lattes, and make a contribution.

List the things you wish you could do. Next to each one, list the next best thing.

1. _____   _____

2. _____   _____

3. _____   _____

4. _____   _____

5. _____   _____

Forgive yourself for not being superwoman. You can always find ways to help, serve, or contribute. They may not be the most valiant or noteworthy, but they're still helpful. Give yourself grace to do what you can, where you are, with what you have. God created billions of other amazing people with gifts and callings; you don't have to carry the entire weight of the world on your own.

GUARD YOUR HEART

Nowadays, our communities extend beyond our neighborhoods, churches, and schools. They can also be found in the little devices in our hands, on computers, and on tablets. Social media has connected the world in ways that were previously unimaginable. Through social networking, we're able to connect with a lot of people and even "follow" others who inspire us. The problem with social media is that it is often a highlight reel of everyday life. It's easy to compare ourselves to strangers on the Internet and to the best styled, perfected, edited, curated moments of their lives. It makes me think of one of my favorite verses from Proverbs: "Above all else, guard your heart, for everything you do flows from it" (4:23). Especially online, your heart needs to be guarded from those lurching feelings of inadequacy you feel when you look at people's profiles or posts. You're in charge of guarding your heart—especially when it's in danger of being pricked so often by something that often seems innocuous.

Give yourself grace to do what you can, where you are, with what you have.

So how do you weed out the bad stuff? Imagine this: the ladies in your neighborhood organize a girls night at someone's home. When you walk into the room that evening, you know a few of the women, but many of them are strangers. One is clearly the popular gal, and people are falling over themselves to take selfies with her. One group of ladies is perfectly polished and put together, talking and definitely not spilling coffee on their designer skirts. Another group is messily eating cupcakes and laughing loudly. So who do you choose to sit with? Our knee-jerk, of course, is to choose the people most like us, the girls who make us feel welcome and at home. And there's nothing wrong with that! We're all trying to build community with like-minded friends. But what if we branched out? Tried saying "You *can* sit with us" to all types of women—and stayed authentic in the middle? We're all just broken girls trying to do life well, cupcakes, fancy skirts, or not.

So why do you follow certain people on Instagram? On Facebook? Does someone else's perfect home make you feel inadequate about your own? *Unfollow.* Does someone else's constant humblebragging about their success make you feel like you're not keeping up? *Unfollow.* Do someone's snarky comments make you feel uncomfortable? *Unfollow.* Do you follow business "competition" just to spy? Do you follow old friends from high school just to make sure you're not missing out on the best new gossip or to feel better about yourself? Are there people on your feed you're not sure why you

UNFOLLOW FRIDAY: *Make your social media feeds places of joy and inspiration. Every Friday, join me in picking a least three things to unfollow online so you can concentrate more on what matters. Mark it on your calendar!*

followed in the first place? *Unfollow.* Distractions, comparison, and negativity be gone! Unfollow relentlessly. Don't let social media hurt your heart with a thousand tiny pinpricks. Make your online world a place of inspiration, genuine connection, and joy. Guard your heart, because what you put in it is what you'll hand out to the ones you love. (While you're at it, make sure *you're* not doing or saying anything on social media that could hurt or alienate others.)

Community is everything, so build it carefully and intentionally.

While we're on the topic of building community and strengthening our villages, it's so important to note the casual contact we have with other members of our communities. Perhaps they're not our closest friends: the server at your favorite restaurant, the receptionist at the nail salon, or the mail delivery person. How can we offer grace and love to those people? We should go out of our way to be exceptionally friendly and loving.

When I was seven, I attended the elementary school where my mom taught fourth grade. After dismissal every day, I did my homework in my mom's classroom and entertained myself until she finished her work. One afternoon, my mom overheard two female custodians cleaning in the hallway. For the first time ever, one of the ladies wouldn't be hosting Thanksgiving dinner because she was unable to afford a turkey. Mom told me what she had heard. Brokenhearted, I asked what we could do to help. So we pooled what was in her wallet and the coins from my piggy bank and headed to the grocery store. We had just enough money to buy the biggest frozen turkey available. Little baggie of money in hand, I trailed behind my mom as she placed the frozen turkey at the register. I counted out the coins and dollar bills and paid for the turkey.

The next morning, we quietly gave our friend the turkey. She was endlessly thankful, but the real magic wasn't in her reaction—it was that a little girl named Emily learned how random acts of kindness can spread love like wildfire. My mom taught me that one of the best things we can do to build community and spread love is to look for needs and find ways to meet them—not just financially but emotionally as well. Mom continued to teach me to look for the ways my love, resources, or friendship could bring good to others. She reminded me to look for people who were alone and to bring them into the group—to be an includer. She showed that impressionable seven-year-old that even small, quiet acts of love—from right where we are, with what little we have—can demonstrate God's love in deeply profound ways and send waves of grace through our villages, further connecting us to our communities. Building community is so much more about looking outward to potential connections than looking inward at our own needs.

Chapter 9

ROUTINES IN RELATIONSHIPS

I sparked with excitement ... at the day that lay ahead, full of endless possibility. Though in a million superficial ways it would be identical to the day before ... my experience of it would be new.

RANSOM RIGGS

ROUTINES, TRADITIONS, AND HABITS take an otherwise mess of a day and bring order, organization, and the safe feeling of predictability to it. So what routines help you feel the most ready for the people in your life and the wild, wonderful, exasperating, and unpredictable things they bring? Maybe you're like me and feel like you can be your best for yourself and your people when you've showered, gotten dressed, and are ready for whatever lies ahead. You're ready for a new day. In fact, at that moment, you're two steps ahead of it. Let's all just sit in that peace for a little bit. You've relieved yourself of the weight of stressors and are ready to serve and love the people in your life to the best of your ability.

Those rare, glorious moments don't happen by accident. Most ordinary human beings do not burst from their cocoons every morning ready to be a blessing to the world. No, these things happen when we set ourselves up for success and remove a bit of frenzy to make space for grace. Think of a time when you felt ready to take on the world because your to-dos were finished. Chances are, you made specific choices to get to that finish line. You made wise choices with your free moments, and little by little, they added up to one deep breath of candlelit air and Febreze.

So how do you take control of your days rather than letting your days get the best of you? Once you trim the fat from your life, you can establish routines for making what matters happen. Then you're left with the precious gift of margin, which you can spend on loving your people.

You might have deduced that tradition, routine, and systems are the backbone of my house. On any given day, a finite number of chores have to be done: lunches to put together, clothes to put on, and beds to make. While not everything always happens perfectly, routines make everyone in my family feel a little more relaxed and a lot less frazzled; everyone knows what's expected of them. Now before we dive in to the routines that work best for our family, let me say in giant letters: FLEXIBILITY IS EVERYTHING.

Inevitably, someone will spill orange juice on his or her new white shirt, the washing machine will break, and an urgent work matter will come up. So keep priorities shiftable. Remember, appointments are reschedulable. Insist that your routines are flexible as well.

To pin down your best routine, begin by defining which parts of life bring you the most anxiety and stress. I'll go first. Mine are mornings (getting everyone, including myself, dressed, fed, and out the door), giving my best to both my work and my family, and the anxiety of never-ending household chores. Establishing routines for each of those areas of responsibility has given me the freedom to feel at peace with my days. Routines also help me manage my mood and anxiety level (which in turn means I'm a much nicer mama and wife). A stressed-out Emily is a grumpy Emily.

> *We're more likely to lose our patience with our loved ones when we're carrying the weight of our stress on our shoulders.*

Let's face it: we're more likely to lose our patience with the ones we love when we're carrying the weight of our stress on our shoulders. Breaking things up

into acceptable patterns allows us to tackle our responsibilities one piece at a time, with managed expectations and clear
timelines.

GOOD MORNING, SUNSHINE: THE
ART OF GETTING OUT THE DOOR

I am *not* a morning person. I'm more of a late-night, get-it-
all-done-while-everyone-is-sleeping person. I love going to
bed knowing I'm waking up to a fresh start, no laundry on
my bathroom floor or dirty dishes in the sink. To make those
mornings happen though, every night before we go to bed,
Bryan and I get ready for the next day. We use our laundry-
basket technique and pick up any "extras" lying around:
clothes, toys, dishes, or trash (see chapter 3). I wipe down
the kitchen counters (and the sink—you were right, Mom!) and
put dishes in the dishwasher. I can confidently say that I sleep
better knowing that even though I may be waking up to a big
work and family to-do list, the household chores are done.

Part of my evening routine also involves a quick beauty
regimen to help prep for the next day. I'll be completely honest here—I wore leggings, my hair on top of my head, and
no makeup for my first two years as a mom. I carried myself
differently when I thought I looked messy or when I felt unpre-
pared to tackle unexpected errands or meetings that might

pop up during the day. But now, when I'm dressed and ready for anything, I can roll with the punches and be flexible with the day.

Establishing a routine is a trick I learned from my mom. The week we brought the twins home, I cried a bucket of tears because I was so overwhelmed with all I had to do. She helped me write out my morning and evening routines (I even taped them to my fridge!) so I could be ready for the day the minute the kids woke up. This, quite frankly, changed my life. Because my mornings had no time for complex primping, I started washing my hair and showering in the evening when I had some uninterrupted time to myself. I picked out an outfit and set my makeup bag on the counter. If I take the time to do these things in the evening, I can hit the ground running in the morning (and sleep as late as possible). Plus, when I devote some time to my appearance, I simply feel better about myself.

The way you begin your day sets the tone for the rest of the day. I wake up an hour before my kids, which is not easy for me but is totally necessary for my peace of mind. When I wake up, I listen to some good music while I get dressed and put on a little makeup. I have disabled all notifications on my smartphone, so I'm not tempted to dive into my inbox before I've had a cup of coffee. Then I launch into that morning routine my mom helped me write out.

Every morning, I grab the laundry from my kids' rooms and my room. It's never much because I try to scoop it up every day. I throw a load of laundry in and make a cup of coffee. I eat breakfast, make Brady's breakfast, and make bottles for the babies. When the kids wake up, I am a much happier mama than if I had stayed in bed and Brady had to drag me out, begging for a bowl of Cheerios. I'm able to deliver so much more grace with my kids when I'm not a frenzied mess in the mornings.

MY IDEAL MORNING ROUTINE:

1. _____

2. _____

3. _____

4. _____

5. _____

It takes a little work, but now that I've been doing it a while, my morning routine has turned into a habit. And now that Brady's old enough, I've given him his own written morning routine:

1. Brush your teeth.
2. Get dressed.
3. Make your bed.
4. Put on your shoes.

He loves this kind of structure because he knows what's expected of him and feels proud when he's accomplished it. Mamas like that feeling too.

THE RULES OF BALANCE

You've heard the term *balancing act*, right? As I said earlier, I'm convinced that the idea of *balance* in life isn't a real thing. It's basically a balancing *act*. No one actually achieves it. Instead, God continually pulls us to and fro, and we have to flow with the changing situation. It's like riding a bike: we're never really perfectly perched on that seat. We're constantly shifting our weight from side to side to keep from face-planting. We could say we're *balanced* on the bike, but we're really in a state of continuous movement and compensation.

And work–life balance? It's more like a push and pull. Here's the thing: I love my work. And I adore my family. I love that I get to have a job I love and a family to care for. But goodness, if it isn't terribly hard to do both. I want to touch briefly on work–life balance here, but we'll dive in to work in depth in the next section. Over time, I've developed a few nonnegotiables that keep my priorities in check and keep me upright on the proverbial bike of life.

1. Family comes first. Period.

2. My work is my ministry. If it takes me away from my family on rare occasions, that's okay. We're all built with an inner gauge for this. When work becomes too teary, too difficult to manage, and too off-kilter, it's time to reevaluate. Hearing my oldest tell his friends that his mom is a "planner maker" gives me a sense of pride in what I'm teaching him about hard work and following a passion.

3. I will be fiercely and unapologetically dedicated to what matters. On top of my short list of what matters: my people.

Set your rules. Creating this structure for your life makes decision-making simpler when the day gets crazy.

Rules:

1. _____

2. _____

3. _____

I haven't found the perfect schedule or routine that helps me "balance" work and family, but I have found that upholding these rules helps me feel confident that I'm giving my best to my responsibilities *and* my loves. Instead of striving for balance in our lives, let's work toward lives fiercely devoted to what matters. That means turning the volume down on the things that distract us from being present.

Here are a few immediate steps to quickly eliminate electronic distraction and help you shift your weight from side to side more easily:

- **Turn off all smartphone notifications.** When I look at my phone and see a number indicating how many unread e-mails I have, it gives me anxiety. So I made all my phone notifications (and pop-ups and text notifications) go away. I check my e-mail when I'm sitting at my desk ready to check my e-mail, not in the grocery store line. I'm better for those people when I give their e-mail my undivided attention.
- **Unsubscribe, cancel, and quit.** Are you distracted by the seventy-five advertising e-mails flooding your inbox each morning? Imagine how much time you could save by simply unsubscribing. Services like Unroll.Me and SaneBox let you unsubscribe in bulk very quickly. Or scroll down to the bottom of that newsletter you never read and hit "Unsubscribe." Need to cancel Netflix or Hulu? Go for it. Don't just turn down the volume on your distractions; turn it *off*.
- **Out of sight, out of mind.** If you don't outright cut those time-suckers out of your life, at least make them less visible. Move social media apps to the

last screen on your phone. Remove shortcuts and bookmarks on your computer. Rest your eyes on things that matter.

We live in a society of *more, faster,* and *extra*. So we feel like we need to respond *more, faster,* and *extra*. But that's a useless exercise. So much joy can be found in slowing down. I fight against my fast-paced, overachieving nature *every single day*. I fight the urge to take on anything and everything. Remember, you have a max capacity. Identify those areas of your life that are overflowing and distracting you, and do something about them. Unsubscribe. Quit. Uncommit. Slow down. Be still. Make revisiting these tasks a monthly routine in your life.

GETTING IT ALL DONE

When Bryan and I were dating, he said to me, "Listen. I have something to admit. I'm really, really good at folding clothes."

"Marry me now!" I said.

A few months later, he actually did, and we lived happily ever after with beautifully pressed T-shirts. (Kidding.) But seriously, did I hit the jackpot or what? Household chores are the nagging argument underlying nearly every relationship I know of. There's always something to be done, and each person always feels like he or she is doing the bulk of the work. But could the solution be as simple as writing them out and dividing them up?

As I mentioned earlier, we used sticky notes to help us split up chores after we got married. Yes, we still argue about chores regularly, but having a system to keep our house clean and our family on track is really helpful. Bryan takes care of the outside, and I take care of the inside. I do what laundry I can throughout the week and wash the bulk on Sunday mornings. He folds it all on Sunday evenings while he watches football. I manage meals and groceries, and he takes care of the yard and fixing stuff. Together we straighten up the house every evening. The split works for us because we wrote down every responsibility and task we could think of and one by one took turns taking a sticky note responsibility. And it has been relatively the same—evenly divided—ever since.

But there is a limit to what even two people can do. Know when it's time to call in the second string. Is there a particular task you're really struggling with? One that's taking time away from what matters most to you? After Brady was born, I found myself cleaning our house every weekend and missing precious time with my kid and husband. Bryan was traveling for work several days of every week, and our time together as a family of three was limited to the weekends. Scrubbing bathtubs and cleaning floors ate into that precious time. We were saving and spending Dave Ramsey–style and didn't have a lot of extra cash. Eventually though, Bryan and I put an actual dollar amount on what that time was worth, and we decided it was better to outsource the deep cleaning responsibilities to a home-cleaning service twice a month. It was hard to swing financially, but it made so much sense for our family. We curbed our eating out and coffee habits and put that money toward this service. Though it was tight, I was much more willing to part with that money than I was willing to part with my Saturdays at the park with my boys.

If it's financially feasible, give yourself the grace to out-source if you need to. You don't have to be and do everything. Ask for help when you need it—even if that means bartering with a friend in a similar situation. Watch each other's children, or help each other clean your homes. Get together for a slow-cooker prep session. Trade your gifts with someone else. Asking for help is not a failure or a weak or wasteful decision. It's a noble decision, and your family will thank you for the peace it brings.

Make a list of chores that constantly drain you:

_____

_____

_____

_____

_____

_____

_____

Does it make sense for your family to consider outsourcing to make more time for what matters? Is there a solution that could bring you more peace?

Routines do just that: they bring peace to our families and homes. A feeling of security comes with knowing what comes next. Though your plans may change, it's certainly nice to know there's a plan in place. I don't stress about the laundry during the week because I know if I do a little bit here and there, we'll get the rest folded and put away on Sundays. I'm not racing to the grocery store three times a week because I keep a list to send to my store on Wednesdays (grocery delivery for the win!). I know I'm going to have clean hair in the morning because I wash it in the evenings. Being able to rest on those plans, however basic they are, makes a real difference in the person I am to my family. Systems and structure like this alleviate some of the stress that turns me from happy Mom into frustrated, can't-keep-up Mom. As my dad always says, if you fail to plan, you plan to fail. An ounce of preparation takes hours of stress and worry from your week—and gives you the space you need in order to give more grace to your people.

RELIEVE YOUR BIGGEST HOME STRESSOR

Which of your household tasks makes you crabbiest? Take a moment to review some of the solutions we've discussed so far, and determine if one of them could free up heart and head space to give to the people you love.

- **Grocery delivery:** Go online and research grocery delivery services in your area. They maybe cheaper than you think.
- **Deep cleaning:** Outsource to a home-cleaning service, or work out a barter arrangement with someone you know. Split the rest of the chores with your spouse. Get your kids involved too!
- **Designate a day to touch base:** Make a new tradition— Sunday coffee with your spouse to coordinate schedules for the week.
- **Daily to-dos:** Write out your to-do list for the next day at the very end of every day. Put it all on paper, and clear your brain for the evening.
- **Write down your daily routines:** Write down every little task that clutters your morning, and see if you can redistribute some of them to the night before. Make a step-by-step routine, encompassing even the smallest things, and stick to it for a week, making adjustments as you go.
- **Simplify dinnertime:** Plan ahead for the week from a list of simple meals your family enjoys.
- **Stock up for impromptu celebrations:** Keep an eye out for party goods on sale. Keep a stockpile to be easily prepared for get-togethers.

Chapter 10

GRATITUDE CHANGES
EVERYTHING

*It is not joy that makes us grateful; it
is gratitude that makes us joyful.*

BROTHER DAVID STEINDL-RAST

MY DAD IS MY HERO. He's strong and kind, and he could
build an entire house by hand if you asked him to. He's the
most giving, selfless man I've ever known. And beyond that,
he's just plain smart. When my family gets together around
the dinner table, we often find ourselves laughing at the way
he can turn a comment about romaine lettuce into a discus-
sion on the iguanas native to Tahiti. Before you know it, he's
rattled off seven species and their Latin names. The man's an
encyclopedia. He's the one I call when I'm worried about a

kiddo's fever or have questions about, well, anything. Basically I hit the dad jackpot.

An avid fisherman in his youth, my dad dreamed of owning his own boat. He finally bought one when I was a teenager. He and my younger brother, Brett, took the boat out for the first time one sunny Florida morning. They'd planned their trip for days, packing just the right amount of bait, the perfect hooks, and the fanciest rods they could get their hands on. They set out on the maiden voyage before dawn. My mom and I couldn't wait to hear how their day on the water had gone. Just a few hours after their departure, though, my mom rushed into my room with a phone in one hand and her keys in the other.

"There's been an accident," she blurted. "Get in the car."

My dad and brother had been having the time of their lives, out on the open bay, when my dad cast a line that got stuck on a buoy. When he yanked the line back to unhook it, it snapped and hit his eye. After multiple surgeries and an eventual full retinal detachment, he's now blind in his left eye.

It was excruciating to see my dad become the victim of such a tragic accident. He is and was our strong and steady rock—knower of all and fixer of everything. While the result of the accident was devastating, my little brother and I learned so much from that experience. We saw my dad dig up all the courage and gratitude he could find to get through one of the most difficult experiences of his life. And he did it all with exemplary strength and leadership.

Day after difficult day, he remarked how grateful he was to have been born with better-than-perfect vision in both eyes so his right eye was able to compensate. He was so proud of my young brother for driving the boat to the dock so he could get to the hospital quickly and for calmly comforting him until we arrived to help. Brett was only fourteen years old at the time. My dad calls that day "the day Brett had to grow up fast." Always the optimist, Dad chose to be amazed by the ways God provided for him rather than focus on the loss of his eye.

PERSPECTIVE IS A GAME CHANGER

Perspective is everything. I believe that God shapes our perspective to soften, strengthen, and bring peace to different parts of our hearts at different times. He guides our hearts to focus on one aspect of a situation for a bit and then refocus on another. It's like using a camera lens—and God gives us the ability to operate the camera. That focus shapes our attitude and ultimately impacts our people in immeasurable ways. Little ones learn from the ways we handle the ups and downs of life. Our friends are discouraged or encouraged by our constant complaining or constant gratitude. We can choose whether to actively focus on tragedy or inadequacies or messes or our weakness or the weaknesses of other people. Or we can choose to focus on all that He's blessed us with—the big and obvious as well as the tiny, hidden pieces of goodness.

We can do this even when things are hard. Yes, my dad lost half of his vision in that accident, but God was working in the hearts of our family and bonding a father and son like never before. Tragedy can truly bond people. Yes, God laid year after painful year of infertility out for my husband and me, but oh my stars, did He awaken my soul to so many beautiful bits of music along the way as He orchestrated an unmistakable song of joy just for us. Yes, God may have you in waiting or may have pulled you through a tragedy in your own life, but the camera is yours. You control your perspective and the state of your heart in the situation you are in today—even when you can't control the circumstances. Choose gratitude and grace every morning. Grace and gratitude go hand in hand.

REFOCUS

When I find myself feeling overwhelmed or downhearted, I try to refocus my camera by actively listing what I'm grateful for. We even started a gallery wall in my house full of framed pictures of answered prayers: a photo from our wedding day, each of our children's first photos, a hand drawing of our house, and pictures of our extended family. Just one glance at that wall puts my heart in the right place. Remembering why

GRACE

and

GRATITUDE

go hand

in hand.

I'm grateful for my people helps draw me out of whatever pit I might be stuck in. It makes me want to be better for them.

What are you grateful for? Big and small, make a list. Here's my list at the moment. I'm grateful:

- for my husband and the way he challenges me and makes me laugh like no other
- for my parents and their exemplary marriage
- that God blessed me not once, but three times with a child
- for a job that I love deeply and a team that inspires me to be better
- that I am healthy enough to enjoy the laughter from my babies
- for the way my oldest is discovering the world

So often I shove gratefulness down into the rabbit hole and tell it to stay there. Why? For insanely silly reasons! Because my house is a mess. Because I don't get a chance to straighten my hair often enough. Because teething is going to be the death of me. *What on earth do I have to be grateful for today?* I ask. I shake my fists at God (again) and ask Him why He's dragging me through this season of life. And you know what He does? He holds my hand as I experience something even crazier. Like getting pulled over for an expired tag (oops) and begging the police officer not to give me a ticket (he didn't, thank goodness) while my bored, always-hungry child sobs from the backseat because we're all going to jail.

When I'm deep in the mess, feeling like everything in life is out of my control, like I'm never going to conquer even a little of my insurmountable to-do list, God always does something to strip me of my excuses for feeling blue. He allows me to walk through my mess and toward a reality check

> *What are you grateful for? Big and small, make a list.*

with little moments of joy and reminders that, even when life is hard, it's good. Through it all, He's with me. He wants me to know that it's never as bad as I think it is. When I finally get over myself and look at my circus from a new perspective, I feel grateful that I *get* to live in this craziness every day.

Consider making your own gratefulness photo wall. What moments would you have represented there? If you don't have a photo of them, what object might remind you of the gratefulness you felt?

The gratitude that wells up from that realization tells me: *I already have all the things I need to live a beautiful life.* Those things are my people. What more could I need? I think about the dinosaur growl Tyler makes when he awkwardly performs his newest skill and claps his two precious, chubby hands together. The way Caroline smiles with her entire face—and her three whole teeth, with a half of another poking through. The way Brady bows his little head of messy, sweaty playground hair and recites his adorable preschool blessing over the food on our table. What more on this earth could I need? No perfect couch, no clean house, no amount of handbags, and no number of followers on Instagram could equal that sweet, pure, relentless joy. With my people surrounding me, the good life isn't so out of reach.

LAUGH TO LIGHTEN UP

We all have a tendency to take life too seriously. We overcomplicate, overthink, and overcommit. Sometimes I think we're all just hamster-wheeling this whole crazy gift of life right out from under our feet. When I feel lost and like I'm spinning out of control on my little wheel, sometimes all I can do is laugh. That's why God gave me my husband, Bryan. He can crack a joke at just the right moment and make the ridiculousness of my plans, worries, and anxieties fall away. I love his ability to instantly take me from a dire situation to a fit of giggles and an eye-roll.

For me, the importance of gratitude is followed closely by the importance of having a sense of humor. What better way to have grace with ourselves and our people than to laugh and let go when life gets too uptight? I used to think I had to make life happen for it to be any good. And as you know, too much focus on that left me exhausted and overworked— too busy nitpicking the day away to find the belly-laugh joy God was inviting me to experience. Missing out on that kind of happiness feels like a travesty.

HUMOR AND HAPPINESS

I grew up on my mom's lasagna and heaping bowls of laughter. One beautiful thing my parents infused our home with was laughter. Both of my parents are quick-witted and always able to find the silver lining or funny element in any situation. After my dad returned to work post-accident, he sat a little stuffed Mike Wazowski on his desk. Mike is the silly one-eyed monster from Disney's *Monsters, Inc*. I suspect that some of his co-workers may have been uncomfortable going into his office for the first time after Dad's partial blindness, but they were soon doubled over in laughter. My dad refused to let the accident take away one of his most precious gifts: his unmatched sense of humor.

Dad's ability to find joy after such a tragedy taught me that God gives grace in so many ways. He gives us humor when it's hard to laugh. He gives us a new perspective when life feels suffocating. And He gives us friends to help us get through the valleys and the peaks of life with comradery and joy. What incredible gifts. My dad's sense of humor helped him connect with his family when we weren't sure what to do or say. It helped turn down the tension just a bit so we could all remember how much we had to be grateful for.

GRATEFUL GRACE

Yes, humor and gratitude work wonders for everyday messes. Yes, they turn things around for us when we choose to refocus our perspective. But what about when you're looking at a long-haul, no-hope situation? When no rose-colored glasses can cover up the hurt and it's going to be a long, painful road to the end? God meets us with grace in those spaces too— when a situation has fallen apart and is out of our control. And His gifts to us there can show us the best part of the human spirit, even in seemingly hopeless times.

When I was a little girl, my grandmother lost her car while shopping at a department store. She walked the aisles of the

MY THOUGHTS

Take a minute to write down three dire situations you're facing right now. Is there a kernal of hidden hilariousness anywhere in them? Is there something to be grateful for that could turn the tide in this situation?

What things bring you the most joy? The deep, sincere, uncontrollable, belly-laugh kind of joy? Make a gratefulness list below.

mall parking lot until security noticed her panicked look and helped her find it. It was the beginning of a heartbreaking road that ended with Alzheimer's. My mom watched as her mother suffered and withered from the disease. I witnessed my grand-mommy, as we called her, forget her daughter's name.

Every Monday, my mom would bake a pound cake for the director at an amazing nursing home in Pensacola. And every Monday afternoon, she would deliver it to him, hop-ing he would agree to admit her mom. I've got to tell you: my mom's pound cakes are incredible. They work wonders. Grandmommy was admitted a few weeks later, thanks to my mom's persistence. From that point on, my mom went to visit Grandmommy every single day without fail, even when it was difficult to see her mother in that condition. I accompanied my mom many times—wearing my prom dress, my graduation cap and gown, and eventually my wedding gown. My mom never wanted her mom to miss out on a thing, even if she was unable to attend these momentous occasions. My mom kept the candy bowl full in Grandmommy's room (for all the nurses, of course) and had a bag of makeup and hairspray handy to get Grandmommy ready for the day.

You see, Grandmommy had always been a glamorous lady. Every Friday of her adult life, she'd gone to "the beauty shop" to have her hair done. In my younger memories of her, she's wearing a fur coat. She took me to fancy restaurants when I was little and taught me ladylike table manners while I wore white gloves. She was a woman of class like no other. And even as my grandmother deteriorated, my mom found the little bit she could do to help—she made Grandmommy beautiful every single day. Talk about showing up and giving grace to your special people, even when it's hard. Grandmommy lived every single day of her life after Alzheimer's like she did before it—with that same beauty inside and out.

Watching my mom go through that experience was incredibly difficult, but she did it with such grace. She was always grateful for the moments when her mama remembered and for the ability to do just a little bit to make her smile—even if it was just lipstick and hairspray. You can take the memory of a woman, but you can't take her spirit. Gratitude changes everything.

I learned a lot from watching my mom serve and love her own mom. I learned that God will fill your cup and give you strength when you physically can't do it. He does it so we can serve and love our people. God's way of revealing Himself to us is by revealing Himself *in* us. When we show God's love and grace, we are living, breathing examples of His perfect love. He gave my dad and mom strength to get through difficult situations by infusing their hearts with everything they needed: gratitude and humor. He will meet you where you are too. That is my takeaway from the past thirty-three years of my life. God desperately wants us to spread His big, unabashed love all over the place. And He meets us in our mess to connect us, strengthen us, and grow our gratitude.

Part 3

GRACE IN YOUR CALLING

WHAT WERE YOU PUT on this earth to do? God designed each of us with a specific purpose in mind. For some of us, our purpose is to invest our time and hearts fully into motherhood. For others, it's to manage businesses that contribute to the greater good of our world. Some were designed to teach and nurture others. Whatever your calling is, God wrote it on your heart when He made you. It can take a long time to discover that calling, and I believe a person's calling can change over the course of her life. Whatever God created you to do, I believe He lit a tiny, flickering flame in you that's waiting to be discovered and fanned. But how do you do that? How do you find, pursue, and execute the job He's asked you to do?

In Luke we're reminded, "Where your treasure is, there

your heart will be also" (12:34). Whatever you can write, sing, or talk about for hours—that is the calling God's leading you to. You were created to fulfill a very specific, colorful, robust destiny, one of great importance. Sometimes your calling is hiding right beneath the surface of daily life, and other times it's a bright, blinking, obvious star guiding your steps as you go. Whatever your calling is, pursue it with your whole heart. Whatever your treasure is, dive into it fully. You were made to be great.

In these next few chapters, we're going to talk through what it means to truly pursue your calling while allowing yourself the grace to do it in a wholehearted and authentic way. We'll uncover tactical ways to trust the journey you're on and how to pick yourself up gracefully when you fall down.

Chapter 11

DEFINE THE LIFE YOU WANT TO HAVE

Your work is going to fill a large part of your
life, and the only way to be truly satisfied is
to do what you believe is great work. The only
way to do great work is to love what you do.

STEVE JOBS

DO YOU REMEMBER WHAT it was like to be fresh out of high school, on the cusp of adulthood? When anything could happen? When we stood at the starting lines of our grown-up lives with seemingly hundreds of roads to choose from? What a beautiful, terrifying place to be. I wouldn't go back there if you paid me! I remember looking around at all my friends who were certain of their perfectly mapped futures. They'd chosen who they wanted to be. Their paths seemed set: doctors, accountants, lawyers, teachers. They'd chosen their hats and wore them proudly, checking all the boxes as they made their way toward their destinies.

I, however, had absolutely no idea what I wanted to do with my life. All I knew was that I wanted the chance to be creative. I wanted to inspire people and make an impact. I wanted to be challenged and pushed. And more than anything, I wanted to be a mama. Essentially I wanted it all—but I wasn't quite sure how to get there. I shadowed family friends at work. I visited my mom's classroom. I even majored in education for a few short months before I realized I was born without that extra-special "thing" teachers have.

I stood looking out at my options, and I felt heavy with worry. None of the roads looked like the one I felt God was paving in my heart. None felt right for me. So one August evening, days before the start of my junior year of college, I gathered up all the bravery I had and changed my major to English. After hitting my knees more times than I can count and asking God to tell me what I was supposed to be when I grew up, I finally decided to look for my treasure—my calling: "For where your treasure is, there your heart will be also" (Luke 12:34).

I didn't know where I'd end up or who I'd become, but I knew I loved books. I loved Emily Dickinson and Ernest Hemingway and Mark Twain. I was the little girl who hid beneath her covers with a flashlight, reading into the wee hours. I loved the way words could paint a story and the way a paragraph could move my soul to feel and experience the depth and breadth of this glorious life. I loved the way writing unleashed my heart and made sense of the world around me. I really believe that God lit a fire in me for writing and wordsmithing *because* He wanted me to follow the path of my passions. So what if those passions didn't lead to a clear-cut career path?

So instead of choosing which hat to wear for the rest of my life, I chose the passionate path of uncertainty. And it was one of the best decisions I've ever made.

I remember nervously sitting down with my parents to tell them I'd declared a new major. I took with me a list of wildly successful English majors to prove that I'd made a good decision. Barbara Walters! Steven Spielberg! Michael Eisner! Surely those names would convince them that their only daughter had made a wise choice. But they didn't flinch. I'm not even sure they read the paper. Instead, they told me they were proud I'd followed my gut. They also told me that if I really wanted to, I could also join the circus.

And there it was. They gave me permission to follow my passion and run full-speed ahead down the path my heart was burning for. That changed my life, and I am so grateful for them and their encouragement. Perhaps it wasn't a perfect path. It wasn't tied neatly in a bow for them to share with their friends. But it was messy, fun, wild, free—and mine. I tell Brady every day that if he really wants to be a cupcake maker when he grows up, I'll be first in line to try every new flavor. I'll even stand outside and wave a big cupcake sign at the cars driving by.

Maybe this is all unfamiliar to you. Maybe no parent ever looked you in the eye and gave you permission to follow your wildly unique, custom-made heart. Maybe you wonder if it's even possible to back up and take another road. Let me assure you: God is the ultimate parent. And as much as I want my boy to follow his crazy cupcake heart, God burns for you even more. So let me say to you what I'd say to my kid:

> Sweet precious one, if one day you are worried about what God is calling you to do with your priceless gift of a life, listen to that heart of yours. Run like crazy down the path God has set your heart ablaze for, and the One who loves you will be around every corner, cheering you on. Be you, little one, and trust that heart God so tenderly gave you. If you don't know what that passion is yet, then keep trying things until it finds you. And in the meantime, you can build a life you dream of.

BUILD A LIFE

Your job is just one tiny part of your life. We talk so much about choosing jobs or selecting careers. But what if we chose a *life* instead? Whether you're seventeen or seventy-five, you can define the life you want to have. Better yet, you can decide how you want to spend your days. God numbered and gave you every single one of those days, so what if you lived each one to its absolute fullest?

Instead of molding your life around your job, choose or create a job that supports and accentuates the life you want to have. Who says you have to work eighty hours a week to be financially or professionally successful? In fact, who says you have to work forty? Who says you have to go to work at 8:00 A.M. and clock out at 5:00 P.M.? You, my friend, have options. You have the freedom to design a life that is beautiful and filling and impactful. Yes, it takes hard work, sacrifice, and planning, but it is possible to create the life you dream of.

Define the life you dream of having. What words spring to mind?

_____

_____

_____

_____

After earning my master's degree in public administration, I ventured off into the corporate world. While I had a few great jobs and incredible titles, I never felt I'd found the right fit. It felt like something was missing. So late one December, I decided I wasn't going to accept the status quo. I wanted something different out of life. I'd moved five hundred miles from my family, and I wanted the flexibility to go home to visit often. Bryan and I were talking about starting a family of our own, and I desperately wanted to give my children the life my mom was able to give me as a teacher with summers and late afternoons off. Being a full-time stay-at-home mom wasn't my calling, but I knew I wanted to pick and choose feathers from all the different hats I could wear. I wanted to make my own crazy, fancy, unique hat.

So I used every millisecond of my spare time to build a business. As I Googled a million questions and watched *all* the YouTube tutorials I could get my hands on, I taught myself to be a graphic designer. While I explored my newfound skills and developed my style, I sold stationery and digital monograms on Etsy. To my delight, I found that brides in particular loved the stationery. I customized it with their initials, and they printed their own DIY wedding stationery and invitations. I sold each monogram for five dollars. I worked in the middle of the night, many evenings until 2:00 A.M., before a 6:00 A.M. alarm sounded the start of another day at my corporate job. Every morning, I'd trade my self-taught Illustrator skills for Excel spreadsheets. I'd swap my topknot and highlighter-covered hands for a skirt suit. But I knew, deep in my heart, that God had a calling for me. And the harder I worked and the more I tiptoed down that path, the clearer God made it.

I sent Bryan a message from my office job every time a sale alert hit my inbox: "Congratulations! You've made a sale!" I still remember the way each of those five-dollar sales was like a direct message from God telling me to keep going—that I could do it. And little by little, mistake by mistake, milestone after milestone, I built a business. God took my itty-bitty dream to build a better life for myself and my family, and He grew it into what is now a major brand of simple day planners, baby books, and home-office accessories sold worldwide.

God molded the mission of our brand out of the desires of my heart. All I started with was the dream to live a unique life and make the most of my days. Now He's helped us create products that help other women to do that very thing. I'm humbled to tears just telling that story. I've made every mistake imaginable and fallen on my face more times that I can count. But through my journey, God has shown me that even though the path is riddled with rocks and mud and muck, the flowers blooming along the path are too beautiful to miss. He's given me strength and courage and patched up my knees more times than I can count.

> *What story is God writing with your life? And how can you lean in to that gentle tug?*

So my question for you is this: What sets your heart ablaze? What story is God writing with your life? And how can you lean in to that gentle tug? This may not mean quitting your corporate job and throwing caution to the wind. It's much deeper than an impulsive decision. God is using you in a very specific and special way. Lean in to your calling carefully and intentionally, and you'll experience something life-changing and life-giving.

FOLLOW THE TUG

To discern where your heart is leading, it pays to spend time on self-discovery. For me, this happens with a pen and paper—pouring my heart and mind onto a blank slate. I love a good Sharpie and a big plain white piece of poster board. In fact, around my office, people like to joke about just how much I love these things. But really: spread yourself out on the floor, and begin to write down the things you love to spend your days doing. Study your big word collage, and look for ways to connect the dots between the common themes.

Now paint a mental picture of the life you want to have. Think about the big and the small. This exercise is great to do every few months as your circumstances change with your season of life. I'll start:

writing	advocating
crafting	assisting
mothering	leading
selling	gifting
organizing	presenting
blogging	knitting
photographing	drawing
designing	painting
building	encouraging
researching	planning
cooking	reading
reporting	noticing
story telling	recording
observing	motivating
volunteering	simplifying
serving	manifesting
number crunching	dreaming
performing	coordinating
loving	supporting
helping	healing
traveling	connecting

I want free time in my days to enjoy my kiddos. I want to be able to be still and quiet enough to soak them in. I want to be able to take the kids to and from school and to volunteer in their classrooms. I also want to do the work I deeply love. I want to work less than forty hours a week while my children are little so I can do the taking to school and volunteering. I also want the confidence and flexibility to travel for work if God puts that in my path. I want to eat dinner as a family as often as possible. And I want my work to inspire my kids to pursue the lives they dream of too. I want to leave a legacy with the way I love people.

It's also helpful to think about the big picture while doing this exercise. Once you know what you want, ask yourself where you want to be in five years. A friend asked me this question a few years ago: "Emily, do you want to A) have a warehouse, twenty employees, a giant printer, and a huge paycheck or B) work from home, have flexibility, make possibly less money, and be small but mighty?"

"B!" I shouted.

The answer was obvious to me, but I'd never actually thought it through. I'd just gone with the flow of daily life, trying to keep up. Now every decision I make for my family and my business comes out of that answer. I want to live a unique life. My goal is not to rule the world or be the biggest planner company on the planet. I want a small but mighty brand that is deeply, wholeheartedly, and fiercely connected to its mission and its community. I want to be both a present mother and a devoted leader. I actually wrote that entire goal out once and taped it to my bulletin board in my office. After that declaration, decision making became a lot easier.

So what are your nonnegotiables? What specific experiences or little life luxuries do you want your family to have? For me, I want Fridays with my kiddos until they're preschool age. Sometimes that means that I have to work late the other days of the week. Though working four days a week is very difficult sometimes, every Friday I spent with Brady before he started preschool is tucked deep in my treasure chest—a little nugget of the good stuff of life. On Fridays, we ran errands. We went to music class. We visited the aquarium. We danced in the car to the Friday Morning Dance Party on the radio at 9:00 A.M. Little Brady and his mama had special Fridays. I didn't fully realize how special they were to me until his first week of preschool. I listened to the Bobby Bones Show Friday Morning Dance Party at exactly 9:00 A.M. after dropping him off at school, and I cried a bucket of happy-sad tears. That special part of my life was over, but

> *What are your nonnegotiables? What specific experiences or life luxuries do you want your family to have?*

good gracious was I glad I'd defined the life I wanted to have early and made those Fridays happen.

I realize taking a day off every week may not be possible for everyone. But don't hold yourself back when imagining the future you want for yourself and your family. What special stepping-stones can you place on the path now to create the life you want to have? I will tell you this: the path isn't easy, but it is so, so worth it.

The path isn't **EASY**, *but* *it is so, so* **WORTH** *it.*

MY THOUGHTS

Describe the life you want to build for you and your family. Don't worry about it being out of your reach. Only after speaking our dream can we try to make it happen.

_____

_____

_____

_____

_____

_____

_____

_____

_____

Chapter 12

GET YOUR HANDS DIRTY

Be undeniably good. No marketing effort or
social media buzz can be a substitute for that.

ANTHONY BOLODKIN

THE FUNNY THING ABOUT owning your own business is that at some point, you wear all the hats. You are the CEO, the cleaning crew, the PR department, the advertising depart-ment, and the secretary all at once. I've been the shipping person and the box-breaker-downer, and I've even pushed pallets up my driveway and unpacked hundreds of boxes in my tiny garage next to our '74 Bronco. But when I first started my business, I didn't want anyone to know that. I set up lots of e-mail addresses like Accounting@EmilyLey.com or PublicRelations@EmilyLey.com. Surely to be respected as a successful business, I'd need everyone to know that I had a giant team in my office running the conglomerate.

I bought a fax machine and a paper shredder and spent tons of money on business cards. I wanted to put all the pieces in place and build the perfect "real business" image to make sure everyone I met understood right away that I had it all figured out. Even as a sole entrepreneur, I used words like *we* and *us* and *our* to keep up the big-company charade. I even used all the money I made during the first two years, without taking a paycheck, and paid for an incredibly trendy (albeit beautiful) website. It was gorgeous. Lots of burlap and white and vintage stamps. Definitely not my preppy happy-stripes-forever style but totally gorgeous. I did it because it seemed like the rest of the world's style at the time. Plus, I needed a slick website to make sure the rest of the world knew my company was large and in charge.

I simply wasn't proud to have a teeny-tiny company. (This was before Etsy was popular and before the maker culture had really started to grow.) I worried that customers would choose bigger brands because they couldn't trust a one-woman show. If I was going to be in business, I thought, I needed to be Kate Spade right out of the gate. Oh, Emily eight years younger . . .

One week before my brand-new website launched, I got an e-mail. A punch-you-in-the-stomach-at-eight-on-a-Monday-morning kind of e-mail. It was very formal e-mail from a lawyer

I didn't know representing a company I didn't know: a cease-and-desist order informing me that my business name (which was not Emily Ley at the time) was trademarked. I would need to change it immediately. I'll never forget staring at my expensive new business cards and my fancy, almost-ready website and realizing that I'd made a grave mistake.

God used that giant bump in the road to direct me toward the real mission He'd set forth for me. I changed my company name to my own name, though at the time I was insecure about the idea. I redesigned my brand and website (slowly and intentionally), let up on the big-company posturing, and put on the warm sweater of true transparency. What a relief. It breathed new, real, and flawed but beautiful life into my brand and into me. I gave myself the grace to be me.

This was the first time I'd ever really embraced my imperfections and shared the parts of me I'd tried to hide for so long—that I had a corporate background (not design), that I was totally self-taught, and that my one-woman-show company was run out of a tiny spare bedroom. I decided that God had given me a message of authenticity, joy, and simplicity—and that it was time to do something with it rather than hide it under all the fluff.

Honestly, though, many times I wanted to throw in the towel. Everyone I admired seemed to be in a stable place, whether in their corporate careers or their entrepreneurial endeavors or their decisions to be stay-at-home moms. But

I was some other kind of animal. I felt alone in this awkward quest to self-teach and develop a brand that felt truly like me. But little by little, this authenticity paved a beautiful way for our company to grow.

After everything, one of the best lessons I've learned is this: everyone has a story about how they started out. Every dream began in somebody's garage or at someone's kitchen table or over two pretty average cups of coffee. Every successful person was new once and had to ask a lot of questions to figure out the way. Every person you admire has accepted help and advice from others and has fallen on his or her face countless times. Show me a self-made success story of a person who's never failed, and I'll show you someone who's telling you a fib.

> *The difference between people who achieve their goals and people who don't is their ability to dust themselves off and wear their dirty outfit proudly.*

No matter what your passions are in this life or what road you're traveling or what goal you're chasing, know this: it's okay to get dirty. It's okay to try one thing, mess up, and try something else. It's also okay to keep trying to climb that same tree, even if you fall down ten times. The difference between people who achieve their goals and people who don't is their ability to dust themselves off and wear their dirty outfit proudly.

INVEST IN PEOPLE

The first year we printed the Simplified Planner, we took pre-orders online and sold more than I ever thought we'd sell. I'd hoped to ship the orders out in December, but at the last minute, my printer told me they wouldn't arrive until February because our volume was more than expected. That's right—February. The planners were printed beginning with January 1. Needless to say, we had hundreds of unhappy, upset customers desperately wanting their planners as they started the new year fresh. I say *we*, but it was actually just *me*—the only employee—answering hundreds upon hundreds of e-mails from disgruntled customers. I thought my dream was over.

About a week before the planners arrived, however, God laid it on my heart that this unfortunate situation was an opportunity. I've always believed that customer service is a ministry. It's a chance to love on people, to over-deliver, and to just do the right thing. And from time to time, it's a chance to restore faith in humanity. So one evening, I got started. I sat on my living room floor with hundreds of gourmet lollipops (delicious ones like vanilla-honey and watermelon-boysenberry), a few black pens, and my dwindling supply of letterpress stationery, and I handwrote five hundred cards. I apologized to each customer, letting him or her know that we'd be refunding part of their payment. And I expressed my hopes that a little treat might make the wait a bit sweeter. We didn't earn any profit on those first planners. In fact, I'm pretty sure we lost money. And that was okay. Sure, I had to work like mad and stay up late and say "I'm sorry" a lot of times, but that experience was magical. At that point, the dollars didn't matter. The sincere connections did.

I can't even begin to tell you what those letters did. Those handwritten notes fell into the first Simplified Planner customers' hands all around the United States, and they connected those women to the brand. I began to see those handwritten notes and lollipops show up on Facebook. My customers were blown away by the way I'd chosen to handle the situation and shared with all their friends online. The gesture had shown them that business can be about more than transactions and receipts. By taking an unfortunate situation, embracing the disappointment, and taking responsibility in a unique and thoughtful way, I sealed the heart of our company. With that first, late batch of Simplified Planners, a very sore hand, and a floor covered in lollipops, I decided my company would be different. Instead of selling widgets and flipping products, I was going to connect with our customers. I was going to make products with heart and authentically serve women desperate for the good stuff of life. And now that the *we* really is a *we*, my staff and I use this idea like fuel for our fire.

Even if the business books say there is a canned answer or solution for every e-mail, comment, complaint, or situation we encounter, we choose to do things with heart. We pour love on our customers and use our customer-service ministry to connect with and serve each person. It's our goal to shine a little light in a negative world. It's not always easy, but pouring love and empathy on other people makes us who we are. It's a way of showing God's love and grace in an otherwise sometimes trite, insincere, and unfeeling world.

The truth is, we all fall down. We all mess up and make mistakes and do and say the wrong things sometimes. But the beauty is in the recovery. It's in the way you handle yourself as you pick up the pieces. It's in having dignity when you're embarrassed. It's in being grateful when you're exhausted. It's in having integrity when you've made a mistake. No matter what path you're on, you know what I'm talking about—you know the pain of face-planting and the embarrassment that comes when you just can't meet expectations. These situations aren't always negatives. Instead, they're often opportunities for us to show what we're truly made of.

What if God has given you a unique set of circumstances—struggles, trials, triumphs, achievements, gifts, and abilities—for

---

REFLECT: *Is there a difficult situation in your life right now that could be an opportunity for you to pour love on someone?*

---

a very specific reason? What if God is gently nudging you to step into your calling? That might not mean making a big career change. It could simply mean living out days that fill you rather than drain you. Maybe stepping into your calling means carving time to exercise and to have coffee with a friend once a week. Maybe the good life isn't so out of reach.

So what are you afraid of? What would it look like to step into a perfectly imperfect life that you were truly passionate about? Would it be worth it to find real joy?

Your desire for a better life has to be stronger than your fear of what it may take to get there. It's as simple as that. Don't put off creating the life you dream of because you're afraid you can't do it perfectly. If you're waiting on your ideal path to open up in front of you, clouds parting and pretty rainbows marking each step, you're going to be waiting a while. Today is the day. That beautifully bumpy road is just waiting for you to take your first step. You were made for this! You will make mistakes. You will fall down. But take it from me: through the ups and downs of owning a business, mothering three children, and being a wife at the same time, I've seen that God is constantly growing us, constantly pruning us, constantly pushing us. It might hurt, but it makes life so much better than before.

Chapter 13

MOMMY GUILT IS A LIAR

*The most important work you will ever do
will be within the walls of your own home.*

HAROLD B. LEE

MOMMY GUILT. IT'S AN EPIDEMIC. The working mom, the part-time working mom, the stay-at-home mom, the super-mom, the room mom, the traditional mom, the modern mom, the helicopter mom, the tiger mom. No one is immune when mommy guilt rears its ugly head to whisper the lie that we're somehow failing our children. We try our best to achieve con-sistent balance—that elusive thing none of us ever actually attains or maintains. We prioritize and say yes to the right things and no to the wrong things. We do the best we can to be the best moms we can be. And still, mommy guilt lives on.

It's a monster, I tell you. And it can totally sabotage our best efforts at living a full life.

Mommy guilt moved into my heart when Brady was born, and it set up camp. The minute he exited my belly, it moved in. I didn't invite it. I didn't ask it to stay. It just hung around and kept creeping back in every time I dug up a little confidence and kicked it out. I had many friends who moved mountains to be incredible stay-at-home moms, and I felt a guilty ache in my heart because I loved my career as well as my new baby. I felt like I was doing something wrong. I also felt like everyone around me was judging my choice to go back to work. Surely giving birth to a child I loved more than life itself meant that I would suddenly want to toss everything else aside, right? But my passions and callings didn't go away.

Here's the thing about mommy guilt: it's born of comparison and life clutter. And every time we listen to it, it gets bigger and louder. It's not just about working or not working. Every choice we make as mothers is an invitation for mommy guilt to speak up. We compare ourselves to perfect-looking mommies on social media. We feel terrible for throwing away the eight-thousandth piece of crayon-doodled artwork that comes home from preschool (never mind that we have sixteen hanging on our fridge). We believe our kids will feel unloved when we secretly don't want to go outside to watch them go down the slide for the hundredth time. Though we bend over backward to make sure our kids know they're loved through and through, we somehow believe this know-it-all—mommy guilt—and let it tell us whether we're doing a good job or not. Mommy guilt gets its power from clutter in our days, insecurity about what matters, and the unrealistic expectation that we can be all things to everyone at all times.

PUT YOUR FOOT DOWN

So how do we turn mommy guilt down? How do we free ourselves from the trap of believing we're not enough? *We simply refuse to entertain it.* After years battling with mommy guilt, I can tell you with certainty that God does not want us to self-sabotage our best efforts by believing these lies:

1. You cannot or should not pursue dreams outside of motherhood.
2. You must pour 110 percent of yourself into your children to serve and raise them well.

No way, friend. No how. I'm stomping my feet and shouting this at the top of my lungs so you can hear it from sunny south Florida: *MOMMY GUILT IS A LIAR.* Yes, God has given us discernment to prioritize and make good choices. But He does not want us to beat ourselves up because we desperately want to take a shower alone.

Quit worrying about whether you're a good mother or not. In fact, here's a handy quiz to tell you definitively if you're doing a good job:

1. Do you love your children?
2. Do you make loving and caring for your people a priority?
3. Are you making the best decisions you can for your family?

If you answered yes to those questions, congratulations! You are a good mom! In fact, you are a *great* mom. You're doing it, sister! Tell mommy guilt to take a seat. Ain't nobody got time for that nonsense.

Pursuing your passions, serving others, doing a job you love, earning an income for your family, taking time away from your children to volunteer or learn or teach or, heck, get your hair done—those are good things. When you contribute and let good things flow into your well, you're not taking away from your kids. In fact, you're filling up with that good, sweet water so you can pour into them later.

On top of that, you are setting an incredible example when you follow your calling. And everyone has a calling. It may be full-time mothering—or volunteering, teaching, exercising, coaching, or pursuing a career. We're not all divided into either the stay-at-home-mom group or working-mom group anymore. It's incredible to see so many mothers modeling true pursuit of passion to their kids, no matter what that passion is. The next generation is going to know that life is worth living *fully*. They're going to know that the little fire God lights in our hearts is worth fanning and sharing. We're going to show that to them.

What makes you whole, unique, and complex?

I never realized what my passions brought to my family until I heard Brady telling people his mommy is "a planner maker who helps people be happy." When Brady sees me excited about something, he learns that hard work and joy are good things. When Brady knows I have to leave the house to do something that doesn't involve him, he learns that the world is a big place and we can make a difference as individuals. When Brady walks into my office and sees samples and swatches everywhere, he knows that creativity is the foundation of growth and that he can do fun things for a job too. It took me a while to accept that I had an identity outside of being a mother. But I've gained so much confidence from it. When we tell mommy guilt to take a hike, we can really enjoy being complex, unique, and special women with lots of valuable hobbies, passions, loves, and responsibilities.

NUGGETS OF GOODNESS AND GRACE

A few nights ago, Tyler woke up from his peaceful sleep with the saddest little cry I've ever heard come over that monitor. When God made Tyler, He made him out of honey and marshmallows. He's just the sweetest little thing. So when he cries, you know he needs you. I put down the laundry I was folding, paused *Parenthood*, and climbed the stairs two at a time. Somehow Caroline was still sleeping, but Tyler was standing at the edge of his crib on his tippy toes with his chubby bottom lip out. I scooped him up and settled down in the rocking chair, careful not to wake Caroline. Tyler loves to find that place where his head can nuzzle into my neck so he can play with my necklace. The necklace was a gift from my husband when the twins were born—a small gold circle representing the completion of our family. Tyler searched my neck for it and rolled it between his little fingers for a few minutes before

When we're still, when we're right where we need to be, God speaks **LOUD** *and* **CLEAR**.

falling back asleep. As I sat there, I felt my heart fill with the warmest, most sincere joy and gratitude. It's in those quiet moments that I feel God telling me, "Keep going, Emily. Keep going. You're doing a good job."

In the war with mommy guilt, God uses small moments like these to give me a tiny bit of confidence wrapped in a deep breath for the next time I need it. That's His grace. That's God giving me just what I need to keep going even though I'm far from perfect. He assures me that all the little choices I've made were for the right reasons. These children He let me borrow from Him are going to be just fine.

> *God gives us gratitude in hidden places.*

In those moments, I feel God's telling me He loves me just as much as I love those kiddos. I'm equally as special. Think about that for a minute. God loves you and cherishes you just as much as you cherish your loved ones. Even more actually. He saves every piece of praise and artwork you create and will watch you go down the slide a thousan times, even if He's busy. And He gives us rocking-chair gifts to show us that He's with us.

For me, that moment in the rocking chair was worth three mani-pedis, two solo showers, and about twelve hours of sleep. (Almost.) It filled me with joy and confidence to counteract that mommy guilt. God's grace pushed it back, turned down its volume, and shut the door to it for a little while. And for about six quiet minutes (until Caroline realized I was in the room and jumped up and down at the edge of her crib to join the rocking-chair party), I was the best mom in the entire world. I'd made all the right decisions. I'd said all the right things. I was on the right path. What a beautiful gift. What a suddenly full well.

We live too many days uncertain of the decisions we're making. But sometimes, when we're still, when we're right where we need to be, God speaks loud and clear.

CELEBRATE THE VICTORIES

God is in the details. In the small victories, the tiny milestones, the little achievements. I vote that we celebrate those things more often than we dwell on the hard stuff or the insecurities.

How do we refocus? I recommend taking time to record your little victories for one whole day. Prayers answered. Moments of peace. Simple solutions. Grateful thoughts. Fill up all the lines on the next page. You're training your brain to cultivate confidence and discover hidden happiness, so think differently. Think outside

> *God is in the details. In the small victories, the tiny milestones, the little achievements.*

the obvious, and delve into the nooks and crannies of your life. You will be surprised what you discover. This is one of the best ways you can edge mommy guilt out and open the door to God's grace. Gratitude changes everything.

Examples:

6:00 A.M.: The kids are still sleeping soundly. I did something right last night. Grateful for a quiet fifteen-minute shower.

7:00 A.M.: Coffee is so good. Grateful for food in the fridge.

8:00 A.M.: Mornings are crazy. I'm grateful I laid clothes out for everyone last night. We were only ten minutes late to school today. Improvement!

God's grace is all around us if we choose to see it. Put on the glasses of gratitude, and you'll be surprised how much your attitude is changed by a new perspective. He's waiting for you to discover Him, to turn down the noise and find the confidence and peace He's offering. You're doing a good job. Keep going.

MY THOUGHTS

Chapter 14

CULTIVATE CONTENTMENT

Contentment: *a state of happiness*
and satisfaction

MERRIAM-WEBSTER DICTIONARY

IN 2009, MY DEAR friend Lara Casey started a movement called Making Things Happen. She was inspired to travel the country organizing conferences to inspire people to dig deep and discuss living life on purpose. And she let me be a part of her team. Together, Lara, our friend and talented photographer Gina Zeidler, and I have traveled from New York to Maui to Chapel Hill and dozens of cities in between. At each stop, we've hosted a gathering of women (and some men) and encouraged them to think about their purpose in life. Being part of Making Things Happen (MTH) has changed my life. But more than that, it has exponentially changed my heart.

I'll never forget attending the very first MTH in WaterColor, Florida, in late 2009. I was an attendee at the time, and I was terribly nervous about making a good impression. I showed up with my fancy business cards, a pocketful of insecurities, and a deep-seated desire to show that my life and business were perfectly pulled together. (Ha!) Little did I know, God had other plans. That experience was like a soothing ice pack on my bruises. I left with a brand-new perspective, grateful tears in my eyes, and twenty-two new friends. Before that, I'd never been in a room full of people who thought like me—who believed that there was more to life than the hustle and bustle. They all wanted to feel deeply alive, make a big impact, and chase enormous dreams. They sincerely cared about what matters most.

I'd found my people. I felt accepted, heard, and understood in those circles of trust. We shared tender stories of family, motherhood, ambition, and service. We opened up about insecurity, loss, heartache, love, and contentment. We were transparent and vulnerable. Simply put, that kind of honesty changes people. Speaking truth is powerful. But despite the overwhelming sense of acceptance, something was bothering me. One of the thoughts we discussed in the room made me uncomfortable.

Contentment. This was a new concept for me, overachieving perfectionist that I am. As I returned to the conference every year, the topic kept poking at me like a pebble in my shoe. Then, during one MTH conference in 2013, my friend Nancy Ray shared what she called her "contentment challenge" experience. While struggling with the need for more, she felt God leading her to put the brakes on her spending. So for ninety days she purchased only necessities like groceries and toiletries. She made room in her heart, home, and life for God to speak more clearly to her. To me, that is the very essence of what simplicity is all about. By simplifying our lives, we're making space for what matters—to hear God more clearly, to give more wholeheartedly, and to place our energy in people and hearts rather than in things. Ultimately, simplifying allows us to slow down enough to savor this life.

> *Ultimately, simplifying allows us to slow down enough to savor this life.*

I had embarked on my own contentment challenge before attending Making Things Happen, when Bryan and I first started dating back in 2007. I decided not to buy a single extra thing so I could pay off three thousand dollars of credit card debt (racked up by chasing the perfect image with the latest trend in designer jeans, all the graphic tees I could get my hands on, and fancy flats). Bryan promised me that if I could do it, he'd take me to Disney World for the day (he lived pretty close at the time). It was terribly hard to break my incessant need for more, faster, better, cuter, and trendier. But dropping the need for the perfect outfit, a perfectly decorated home, and perfect accessories changed my heart. Much like fasting from junk food, it cleansed my system of the need for more. Plus, it helped me focus on the things that really matter by freeing me from online window shopping and "stuff" envy. And I got to go to Disney World. It really was a win-win.

We're members of one of the most privileged societies in the world. So why do we yearn for more when we have so much already? I feel uncomfortable even writing about it because I'm still dripping in disobedience and greed. Tens of thousands of people every day die from hunger, yet we're throwing out food we forgot about because we had so much other food to eat. Countless kids around the world will never learn to read, yet our children's bookshelves are overflowing with books we haven't gotten around to opening yet.

Where do you see yourself overconsuming? Keep track of your spending over the next week, and meditate on the stuff you waste the most on. What hole might you be trying to fill?

We have so much. We have education, food, shelter, knowledge, technology, opportunities, access, abilities, and talents. But still, for reasons carved deep into the walls of our hearts, we want more, better, faster. We glorify a chronic breakneck pace, always moving forward, always upgrading, adding, and amassing. But what if, even for just a few days, we addressed the perfectionism that produces these ugly feelings? What if we took a good look at the burning holes in our hearts to see what they are *really* shaped like?

Is the hole we're filling really shaped like a new dress or a new pair of shoes? I don't know about you, but I had a baby-shaped hole in my heart for a long time. I tried to fill it with dark-wash skinny jeans, knickknacks, and more stuff from Target. I remodeled our entire kitchen trying to take my mind off it. White subway tile didn't get me very far. Do you know where it did get me? To a sad place where all I wanted was all I'd never have. I had to address the real ache. I had to free my always-outreached hands, which were waiting for the next adrenaline rush spurred by the joy of holding something new.

SIMPLY CONTENT

Contentment plays an enormous role in our ability to simplify. In fact, it's the very foundation of the concept. Imagine what life would look like if we were truly content with just the objects we own. Sit on that for a minute. *All you have now is all you'll have.* That thought makes the kitchen table I want to replace look pretty good. *Merriam-Webster* defines *contentment* as a state of happiness and satisfaction. Yes, please. I deeply want that kind of peace. Just like the pages in our planners, our lives could use more white space. More emptiness—physically speaking. When we rid ourselves of excess, we make room for God.

EXCESS

Tactically, how do we rid ourselves of excess? How do we pursue the heart-change we're after? Our mailboxes are full. Our inboxes are full. Our closets, pantries, bookshelves, and cabinets are full. Our *lives* are full. How do we expect to fit in time for playing on the floor with little ones? Or date nights without cell phones? Or new, serendipitous discoveries with friends? All the excess overshadows the important stuff.

Every possession we have is a window to our heart—an opportunity for something to impact us. That includes every e-mail, every computer file, and every piece of junk mail that steals three seconds of your time. Add those up *and remove them*, and you've got fifteen minutes to sit by yourself in a tub and read. You get your life back, minute by minute. And that's no small thing.

How can you find real contentment? Start with three steps: clear the clutter, fast from distractions, and reshape your heart with new focus.

Clear the Clutter

- **Inbox:** Visit Unroll.Me or a similar service to unsubscribe all at once from e-mail subscriptions and newsletters. Adopt the Flag-or-Trash e-mail system: end every day at zero by flagging e-mails that need attention and deleting the rest. No need for lots of folders or color codes. Red flag or trash. That's it. When you have time, address flagged e-mails. You do not need to work in real time, answering e-mails on your phone or computer the minute they're received.

- **Mailbox:** My mailbox is slam full every single day. And after all the time it takes to sort through the paper, I end up throwing most of it out. Visit CatalogChoice.org, DMAchoice.org, or another such service to opt out of catalogs and junk mail lists to decrease the amount of mail you receive. That's a little more brain space you've taken back.

- **Computer:** Do your files and systems make you feel overwhelmed? Adopt a very simple system. I love Dropbox for accessing files from any device. Several other cloud-sharing systems do the same thing. I have one folder on my desktop with three folders inside: Personal, Work, and Photos. Now, each one has a gazillion folders inside, but they're organized so that finding files is quick and painless.

- **Phone:** Move apps you don't use regularly to a place

on your phone where you can't see them. On the start
screen, keep only the apps you use daily, even (and
especially) if those apps don't fill up the entire page. Ah,
breathing room. Delete apps you don't use.

- **Stuff:** We talked about physical possessions and all the
things we own in chapter 3. Be relentless with your trash
pile and donate pile. Physical clutter is mental clutter.

Fast from the Distractions

- **Social media:** Social media can be a great thing
to keep us connected and inspired. It can also be
a ginormous time-suck and a breeding ground for
comparison. Remember: unfollow, unfollow, unfollow.
If someone makes you feel icky or insecure inside,
why follow that person? Make your feed a place of
inspiration and encouragement. Find accounts that are
uplifting and authentic, and feed your brain with that.
I follow two accounts on Twitter: Bob Goff and Love
Does. That's it. It's a happy feed full of balloons, Jesus,
and perspective. Every once in a while, fast from social
media to get some perspective back. Start with a
certain time of day, then maybe a weekend. Eventually
new habits will form, and the fear of missing out
(FOMO) will fade away.
- **Online shopping:** Do you window shop online?
Remove those bookmarks. Clear your Internet history.

Unsubscribe from those sale alerts. Find a new way to give or save that money.

- **Excessive commitments:** Just say no. Free yourself from the trap of being spread too thin. Quit something. Refer back to chapter 4 for a refresher.
- **Media:** We've put a limit on TV and technology at our house, but it's still something we struggle with. Primarily, I struggle with noise. There's always a ping or a ding or a notification or an announcer on as the soundtrack to my life. But I don't want to hear that! I want to hear baby giggles, my five-year-old's discoveries, and all about my husband's day. Turn off the notifications on your phone or tablet. Put it in a drawer if you have to. Throw it out the window even. Make the mute button your favorite button on the TV remote.
- **Other:** What else is holding you back? Write out what's keeping you from finding real contentment in your life. A Target addiction? (They have Starbucks in there! I get it!) Too many episodes of *Gilmore Girls*? (← I *really* get that one!) Comparison? Self-doubt? What can you fast from?

Give Your Heart New Focus

- **Rest:** Sleep recharges our bodies and refreshes our souls. As a society, we've lost the ability to be still in our minds. We take our phones to bed with us and find every reason in the world to fill our hands and minds with stuff. Practice the art of stillness without distraction. I remember someone telling me once that if our children always see us with our hands full, checking phones at red lights or multitasking during playtime with them, we teach them it's not normal to simply sit, stare out the window, and sing along with the radio. We teach them that simple is boring. So rest. Be still. Let your tank fill itself while your body refuels.

- **Read:** Allow your mind to wander. Reading does great things for me. It takes my brain out of work and child-rearing and into new places, new situations, new problems I don't have to solve, new experiences, and new people. Read a novel, and give your imagination a workout. Or go nonfiction and learn more about the world you live in.

- **Listen:** My dad says, "God gave us two ears and one mouth so we'd listen more than we talk." Hear the stories your children tell. Hear the sounds of your family and your home. Hear the voices of your friends and neighbors and the songs of the birds outside. Soak in the sounds of your beautiful life.

Finding contentment is as much about simplifying as it is about changing the attitude of your heart. Contentment is a practice, and it's worth taking up consistently. Rid yourself of excess, fast from distractions, and refocus your heart. You'll find that joy is already in front of you, just waiting to be recognized.

Chapter 15

LOVE YOUR SEASON

Embrace this season of life, for
it is just that . . . a season.

ONE EVENING IN EARLY 2015, Bryan and I were watching *The Bachelor* on TV. (Don't tell him I just outed his love for *The Bachelor* and *The Bachelorette* to the world.) I checked my e-mail on my phone during a commercial and saw something that quickly sent us into a tailspin. It was from a producer from the show *Shark Tank*. Yep, that *Shark Tank*—where new entrepreneurs compete for backing from investors. I'd applied for the show on a whim after our Simplified Planners had sold out in mere days a few months prior. We had so many customers asking for planners that we just didn't have enough to go around. What a great problem to have! But still, it was a problem we couldn't solve, and I thought the show might help us toward a solution.

The producer's e-mail said she'd like to give me a call for an impromptu pitch in fifteen minutes. Was I available?

Was I available! I jumped from my chair and quickly came up with answers to the questions she might ask, and then I gave her a call outside on my patio. *Shark Tank*! Unbelievable! Of course I wanted to go on the show. That enormous step forward would mean great success for our company, right? I saw a green light, and I went full-speed ahead. I pitched the producer, and she loved our company and situation. She asked me to send a video pitch so their team could review it.

Years deep into our journey with the Simplified Planner, we always faced the wonderful problem of selling out. Every single time. Sometimes in just minutes. Dedicated to our commitment to run a debt-free company, we ignored others' advice to take out a small-business loan to make bigger production runs. We had committed to running our company with cash in hand. When the *Shark Tank* opportunity presented itself, we viewed it as an obvious next step for growth. We would finally have the money to print enough planners! Sure, we'd take on an investor (hopefully), but we'd get bigger and bigger and bigger! What wasn't to love about that idea?

We decided to share our real life with the producers, since authenticity and transparency had always been a cornerstone of our brand. Bryan and I attempted to film a video with my iPhone balanced on concrete blocks at the building site of our new house, which was still in the framing stages. Great setting, right? Terrible idea.

Enter God, telling me at every corner that this was not our path.

Bryan and I filmed the first take (cue Tyler crying). Bryan and I filmed the second take (cue Caroline hungry). Bryan and I filmed the third and final take (cue Brady throwing sand above his head and spinning in circles behind the camera. Cue sand in his eyes. Cue tears.) We gave up and got in the car. I felt unbelievably frustrated with my season of life in that moment. I was silent the rest of the way home.

That evening, after the kids' bedtime, Bryan and I had a chance to talk about what the *Shark Tank* opportunity would look like if it actually did happen: an inventory, debt, an explosion of orders, reality TV notoriety, another owner who may not share our values. In short, God closed that door for us and told us to keep going down the path we'd been on.

> *The peace of contentment is just as valuable as the confetti that comes with achievement.*

We were exactly where we should have been: debt-free and content. Through this experience, I realized that the peace of contentment is just as valuable as the confetti that comes with achievement. God reminded me that this season in our lives would soon be over and a new one would come. The timing wasn't right for us to be on the show, but He was still going to take us places if we stuck to our guns.

That year we saved every business penny we could. We emptied our business savings account and printed thousands more Simplified Planners than we ever had. I was honestly scared we'd be sitting on piles of them at the end of the year. It was a brave and big move. And on New Year's Eve 2015, minutes before a new Simplified Planner year, eight of our nine editions had sold out. It was our best year ever. God has a way of making our seasons make sense, doesn't He? Sometimes it just takes a little bit of leaning in to realize that even if life doesn't look as glamorous as it could, His beautiful plan is still at work. We made the right move for our brand, our team, and our family and haven't looked back.

WHEN WILL I WASH MY HAIR AGAIN?

Does this sound familiar to you? You're pursuing your calling. You're managing family and kids and parents and friends and, I don't know, taking a shower every once in a while? You haven't washed your hair in a week, and you're not quite sure when you last shaved your legs. One kid's tossing your lukewarm coffee across the room. One kid's crying and begging for more Cheerios. *Do we have any more Cheerios?* you wonder. One kid's kicking the arm of the first kid like it's a game.

First name, middle name, last name! Don't you dare! Your counter is covered in mail and three Target bags. Your phone is buzzing, and your inbox is dinging, and your to-do list is so long you can't see the end of it. You wipe your hands on your pants because you're out of paper towels (*rats!*) and realize your hands were covered in applesauce and highlighter. *I give up.* You lose your temper with somebody before throwing in the towel and throwing everyone into the bathtub so you can sit with your back next to a wall and cry into your second cup of lukewarm coffee while making sure they don't hurt each other.

This isn't how it was supposed to look . . .

Stop right there. How is it *supposed* to look? When we create fantasy images in our heads, we slay the beauty in our lives. Comparison truly is the thief of joy. And we've established that standard of perfection in our work and our families based on what? Social media highlight reels? Perfect people? (I'm telling you—they're like unicorns. They don't exist.) Being a woman with many loves and responsibilities will test your patience, stretch your will, and make you love more fiercely than you ever thought possible—because time is your most precious commodity. Remember, though, that this part of life—this busy, crazy, circus-like place you're in—is but a season. It will come and go just like all the others.

Let some things slide. It's okay if you don't wash your hair for a week at a time during this phase. (That's what dry shampoo and top knots are for!) There will be plenty of other times to be that kind of beautiful. Now is the time to be

> *When we create fantasy images in our heads, we slay the beauty in our lives.*

another kind of beautiful. Now is the time for patience, gracefulness, four books before bed, thoughtful communication, adventures, and being a master at Candy Land.

Sure, you count the minutes until bedtime, but as soon as their little freshly washed heads hit the pillows (hey, at least someone has clean hair), you start to think back on the day, relishing their tiny personalities. And sometimes you scurry about your workday, checking off to-do list tasks, bouncing from meeting to meeting, just waiting for the clock to strike five. It's okay if it's date night and all you do is eat your chips and queso in silence and enjoy a little face time. Go with it. Just keep doing what you're doing. It's fine if your dresser drawers look like they've been hit by a natural disaster. Are you still able to find things? Awesome. Do what works. Forget the rest.

Right now I'm sitting at my computer for the umpteenth night in a row, escaping my own little circus to write a book. And here at the end of it, I'm certain that my best advice to anyone facing this craziness is this: soak it up. Give in to the crazy. Because without it, you won't find real joy. You'll find styled joy. Staged joy. Perfect joy. No thanks.

Do what

WORKS.

Forget

the rest.

Cultivate realness in this season. Embrace the bumps in your road. Invest in dry shampoo. Purchase a cordless vacuum cleaner, and teach your littles how to use it. (Seriously. They'll love it.) Build structure and routine, but build it ever so loosely. Bedtimes are important, but kids won't always scream for you to crawl in bed with them. Teaching your kiddos independence is important, but your little girl won't always poke that bottom lip out and make grabby hands at you. (Well, maybe she won't.) Work won't always be so frantic. Enjoy being needed and sought after. Your friends won't always knock your door down begging for a coffee date. Make time. Savor the fellowship.

I have strong convictions about the type of life I want to live, but I must face the fact that during this season of life, with three kiddos under five, it's possible only in bits and pieces. God is changing my heart and challenging my resourcefulness. I know very well that He wants me to walk intentionally through this life and not skip along the path blindly. There are lessons and memories and stories to be found here, and I'll take what I can get.

This stage of your life may be difficult. It may bring you to tears at times. Perhaps God has you in waiting for children, or maybe He has you in the thick of divorce or tragedy. Some seasons are particularly hard. No matter the season, let this cold winter or this hot, crazy summer wash over you. Grieve if you need to. Call on your people. Embrace the joy of small pleasures. Sit amid the piles of toys. Let the kids be kids. Brady loves to throw his stuffed animals from the balcony at our house. I know he is going to hit my favorite blue lamps one day. But instead of putting an end to the second-story pitching, I've coached him to one side of the rails. He has but one childhood. And this is its time. Work your fingers to the bone until seven o'clock. Whether or not you love your job, let your gifts shine, and share them with the world.

I'll freely admit that I don't always know what to do in the middle of all the chaos of work and family and life and friends. When I'm completely overwhelmed with it all, I sometimes lie on my back and let the kids play all over me like puppies. Then, staring straight into the heavens, I think, *What would my own mama do?* She led, loved, and shepherded our family with such grace. True, many of my childhood birthday parties were magazine-worthy. But magazine photos are not really what matters. She loved with real love, not styled love. She and my dad allowed us to be kids by embracing the season we were in. By leaning in and loving big. Oh, how I want to do the same.

LEGACY

One day we'll add up all our seasons—the joyous ones, the heart-wrenching ones, the momentous, average, and peaceful

You, just as you are,
are **ENOUGH**.

ones. When we do, we'll have one rich life story. An illustration of faith and doubt, grace and worry, friendship, learning, and loving. Each season connects to the next with links of growth and change. At the end of our lives, we'll each look back at that chain of experiences with meaningful stories to tell. We'll unpack nuggets of goodness from our pockets and pass on hard-earned wisdom. Sure, we may have scars from the countless times we bit it, but we'll be really good at standing back up. That, friends, is what legacy is.

What will your legacy be? How often have you considered that the perspectives you have will be passed on to your children? The way you let go of mommy anxiety will be handed down to your daughters. The love you give away to the world will be reflected on your children, and their children, and their children after them.

We have a gift right now, in this moment. It's an opportunity to welcome God's grace and to free ourselves from the traps of self-labeled inadequacies. Now is your chance to tell yourself the truth: You *are* measuring up. You *are* doing a good job. You, *just as you are*, are enough. Enough for yourself. Enough for God. And enough for the ones you love.

As my grandmother would say, be still, sweet girl. Be still and listen. Let God's truth resonate in your life *just as it is*. Not one day when your house is clean. Not one day when all the laundry is put away. Not when the time is right. But right now.

God's grace is all around you, settling on and highlighting little joys and tiny blessings we may not always see.

What will all your seasons add up to? What legacy will you leave? I dream of building a business founded on unapologetic, whimsical love. I dream that my legacy will be loving, creative, open, accepting, and fierce. Your dreams can become your legacy.

Here's one last exercise. Sit, palms up, with your eyes closed. Sit and listen. What story will you live? Many of your seasons are yet to be defined. That next link in the chain is totally up to you. Is it grace? Trust? Faith? Growth? Choose your next step. Joy is found in the journey—a journey of simple and profound grace poured constantly on perfectly imperfect women like you and me. This is your time.

God's **GRACE** *is all around you.*

THANKS

BRYAN—THANK YOU FOR LOVING and encouraging me and my wild, crazy, passionate ways. Thank you for leading our family and stewarding my heart in ways I never could have dreamed of. Thank you for pushing and challenging me to be my absolute best. Thank you for making my life a beautiful adventure. I'm honored and grateful to do life with you, B.

Mom—thank you for being the ultimate example of what a mama should be. Thank you for sacrificing and giving and building and creating and loving endlessly so Brett and I could live lives full of joy. Thank you for crossing every *t* and dotting every *i* in the name of thoughtfulness. I remember every single one. They made me who I am.

Dad—thank you for telling me I could live any life I wanted. Thank you for encouraging me to be me and to chase my crazy dreams. Thank you for showing me, with gummy bears and fishing rods no less, that life doesn't have to be standard—that it can be lived big and loud and fun. I want to be just like you when I grow up.

Brett and Taylor—thank you for cheering me on and encouraging me every step of this crazy way. I love you both dearly and am so proud of the people you are. My kids are the luckiest to have family like you.

Lara Casey, Gina Zeidler, Natalie Norton, Rhi Bosse, Amber Housley, Kristin Winchester, Nancy and Will Ray—your friendship means the world to me, and I'm so grateful for the ways you point me back to the Lord and His goodness at every turn.

Gina Hafley, Brittany Werth, McKenzie Fussell, Whitney Hawkins, Hannah Myer, and Dusty Pyatt—thank you for championing this mission and loving me through the good and hard parts. Thank you for being women of courage, integrity, and deep, wholehearted love. God spoiled me with you five.

Lisa, Dusty, Amy, McKay, Pardis, Elisa—thank you for being our family away from family. xo

Hannah Myer—thank you for helping me love my children well and steward their precious hearts. You are an endless blessing and an incredible friend. Because of you, I've been able to be my best at what the Lord's called me to be the past few years. I love you dearly.

Megan Cate—thank you for helping me through motherhood. Sleeping babies are everything.

Evelyn Rodriguez—thank you for your friendship, your example of godly motherhood, and your amazing burrito bowls.

Brady—you, my sweet boy. This book is for you, punkin' pie. You are my sunshine and my everything. God made all my dreams come true with you. You are strong and smart and creative and brave. I am so proud of the big boy you are becoming, and I thank God every day for allowing me the privilege of being your mama. Thank you for being you, B. Go and do and be all the things you want to be, Brady Bear. I'll be there cheering you on from the sidelines every step of the way. I love you more.

Tyler—my sweet middle baby by three whole minutes. God made you out of marshmallows and honey. He broke the mold when He sent you to us. Thank you for being the epitome of sweetness, my little monkey, and my kiddo with the best dinosaur roar. I love you to the moon and back, and I can't wait to see who God shapes you to be.

Caroline—my darling girl, my one and only. God knew what He was doing when He made you of cinnamon and sugar. You are silly and sweet, and you smile with your entire face. Nothing on this earth compares to your smile. One day, when you read these pages as a mama yourself, I pray with every inch of my heart that you'll take a breath and let God's grace wash over you. You are worthy and special and perfect *just as you are.* I love you, Caroline Sue.

To Donna, Nicole, Auria, Chris, Amber, and all my friends at our local Starbucks—thank you for making a little makeshift home for me every evening between bedtime and closing while I poured my heart into this book. I am forever grateful for your friendship and caffeine. But mostly your friendship.

To our Simplified Planner community—thank you for your dedication to the good stuff of life. Your Instagram encouragement and support of our brand and of each other stirs my heart daily and makes me so incredibly grateful for the honor of doing this work. I'm so inspired by you.

Gina Zeidler, Shay Cochrane, and Laura Foote—thank you for capturing the incredible photographs in this book. Your work is so incredibly special.

To my incredible book team—thank you, from the bottom of my heart, for guiding me through this process with love and care and for giving me the chance to put my heart on paper.

ABOUT EMILY LEY AND THE
SIMPLIFIED PLANNER®

EMILY LEY is a designer, wife, and mama to three precious, wild little ones. Raised in Pensacola, Florida (home of the most beautiful beaches you ever did see), Emily graduated from the University of West Florida with degrees in English, marketing, and public administration and went on to become the executive director of the city ballet. From there, she worked in nonprofit management and public relations before launching her brand in 2008. In 2011, after the birth of her first son, Emily created The Simplified Planner®—a simple agenda for busy women like herself. Following the success found at its online home, EmilyLey.com, the brand quickly grew to be carried in over 600 retail outlets across the United States and around the world. Emily enjoys Friday pizza parties on the living room floor, hunting down the best queso in the world with her husband, and making memories to savor for a lifetime with her twins and preschooler.

Connect with Emily on Instagram at @EmilyLey, where she shares snippets of her family, behind-the-scenes of her business, and occasional heartfelt insights. Visit EmilyLey.com to see more of the Emily Ley brand.

The Simplified Planner® is a beautiful, joyful agenda for busy women in all seasons of life. Designed minimally on purpose, its open pages serve as a fresh start every day. We don't just make planners. We make purposeful tools to inspire, equip, and empower women who deeply desire more joy and simplicity. We believe margin matters, and our mission is to inspire women to organize, simplify, and carve white space for the good stuff of life.

Connect with The Simplified Planner on Instagram at @SimplifiedPlanner for daily inspiration and simplicity tips.

Visit the Resource Library at EmilyLey.com for free printables, e-books, webinars, and more content for pursuing a life of joy and simplicity—embracing grace, not perfection, along the way.